All in a Lifetime

by

Matt Lethbridge, BEM

GW00771592

Printed by Pryntya Limited, Cornwall, TR16 4AX. Tel: 01209 202190
Published by Matt Lethbridge

'St. Eia', Hugh Street
Hugh Town
St. Mary's
Isles of Scilly

ISBN 0-9545250-0-0

CONTENTS PAGE

ACKLNOWLEDGEMENTS

I would like to pass on my sincere thanks to Frank Gibson for his permission to use many of his photographs and also to R.N.A.S. Culdrose for their permission to use the aerial shot of the *Guy and Clare Hunter* when she was on service to the Fastnet Race yachts.

Introduction

Matt has asked me to write a short introduction to this book. I find it a great honour that he should ask a fellow islander to do this.

I have known Matt all my life and have been truly astounded at his dedication to the lifeboat service in these islands. He followed a great family tradition with his father and grandfather both being coxswains. His dedication meant that he would not take a holiday in case of missing a service and he was only inveigled away on false pretences so that Eamonn Andrews could have him on his 'This Is Your Life' programme. Matt's first reaction when he saw a lot of his crew on the stage was, 'Who is left home to man the boat?'

During his period of service he was awarded three Silver medals, as well as numerous vellums and framed certificates for his bravery and outstanding seamanship.

Since retirement he has become an excellent painter of ships and shipwrecks in Scilly. The backgrounds to the paintings are all done from memory, which shows his uncanny knowledge of the scattered rocks and islets where the ships were wrecked.

No dedication would be complete without mentioning his wife Pat, to whom he has been married for over 50 years. The women of the lifeboat crews could be called the silent service of the R.N.L.I. They sit and wait for hours whilst their loved ones are away on service and Pat has been a constant source of strength to him.

Matt has become a legend in his own lifetime and I personally recommend his story to all lovers of these islands and to those further afield as an example of those in peril on the sea.

Frank Gibson

Frank Gibson
St Marys, Scilly 2003

GLOSSARY

A.R.P. .... Air Raid Precautions

A.S.R. .... Air Sea Rescue

A.T.C. .... Air Training Corps

C/O .... Commanding Officer

Cox .... Coxswain

D/F .... Direction Finding

E.T.A. .... Estimated Time of Arrival

L.A.C. .... Leading Aircraftman

N.C.O. .... Non Commissioned Officer

R.M.L. .... Rescue Motor Launch

R.N.L.I. .... Royal National Lifeboat Institution

R.N.O. .... Resident Naval Officer

T.H.V. .... Trinity House Vessel

W/O .... Warrant Officer

Chapter 1

Family

AFTER MANY suggestions that I should record some of the things that have happened to me – how do I start writing about my life? I suppose firstly I have to tell of my family.

On both sides of our family, my father and my grandfathers were fishermen. My grandfather on Dad's side, Jim Lethbridge, went away to sea as a young boy, and was at the age of nineteen, as far as I have always been told, a bosun on a four-mast barque. After returning home to get married, he settled back in his birthplace, to spend the rest of his life as a fisherman, boatman and lifeboat coxswain in about 1914.

My grandfather, Richard Harry, on Mother's side was a St. Ives fisherman all his working life, living in St. Eia Street and used to tell of chasing the herring shoals in one of their luggers all around the coast. They would start to fish up the West coast of England, crossing to Ireland, back up the West coast to Scotland, around the top and down the East coast to Scarborough and Whitby, down to Plymouth and Mount's Bay then back to St. Ives. I spent many, many hours with him out in the punt fishing, or in our garden fixing the chicken sheds leaks, with sheets of brown paper and tar. He was also a great gardener, only vegetables as I remember.

Grandad Harry and Me.

The last time I remember going fishing with him I must have been about seven years old and my mother had told him the year before that he was too old to be going out in the boat, so this particular Saturday morning being not a school day, he said to me, 'I will clean the chicken house on my own this morning, you go down to Porthcressa beach and dig some lug worms for bait, we will be going fishing after dinner (midday), but don't tell your mother.' So I got the worms in the late morning and we were out in the back yard baiting up the spiller, which is a long line of usually about 100 hooks with a weight at each end. The next we knew Mum arrived and immediately started telling Grandad off, but he was ready for it and he just looked at her and said, 'Well what could I do, the boy has been down and dug the worms, so what else could I do?'

I did not ever get seasick and so in the school holidays I was always allowed to go out in the fishing boat with Dad and Uncle Jim, unless it was poor weather. Also I used to go out with Dad for the day in the *Kathleen* (a sailing boat), in which after going out for the day for lobsters and crayfish at around 4 am in the morning and returning about 9–9.30 am, he then had a quick bite to eat and took people line fishing or landing on some of the uninhabited islands. I remember the first time he left me in the *Kathleen* on my own, she was at 32-foot yawl with two headsails, a main sail and a mizzen sail, and we had as a passenger an ornithologist. He wanted to land on a rock where a peregrine falcon was nesting.

On arrival off the rock, my father altered the set of the sails and set off to land the gentleman in the rowing boat, saying to me as he went, 'Look after the boat boy.' So I, a six or seven year old boy was just left in the boat with no anchor down and worried sick the boat would sail away. My Dad of course knew that as long as I used my head and kept calm the boat would not go anywhere while the sails were set as they were, but it taught me an important lesson – how to heave the boat too, so that she could be left with minimum movement while you were otherwise engaged.

Dad never did tell me a lot but he expected me to watch and take notice of all that was happening and by doing so I would never forget what I had learned that day. For instance, he would say, 'Here take the tiller,' which was the rudder control and then he would stand in the front not telling me where we were going, but I would have to think for myself. For example if the wind was from the West he was most likely going to the West, South West or North West. The reason, I realised after a while, was that if we went West into the wind, if the weather turned bad or the wind went off, we had a fair wind home. I also began noticing what state of tide it was when we went to different places to fish, if I got it wrong all he would say was, 'Where do you think you're going?' with a bit of a dark look which meant, 'You should know better.' This was a great way of teaching really, I remember many years later we were out among the rocks in the motor-boat and I asked him what were the transit marks to go through a narrow passage between some rocks. He turned and said in a bit of a growl, 'Now look boy, forget about bloody marks, you can't see marks in a fog or in the dark, but just remember where the rocks are and how close you can get without hitting anything, then in fog or at night you can find your way from rock to rock and in fine weather you know where it's safe and where it's not.' That lesson was one of the most important to me in later years. Another thing he said when I asked him the name of some small rock somewhere was, 'Look boy the name of the bloody thing don't matter as long as you know where it is.'

All through my boyhood days from before I can remember, the sea and boats controlled my life. I was told many times that the first, but not the last time I fell overboard I was only eighteen months old and was out in the punt with my cousins, Evelyn and Jack, and my Aunt Bessie. I was holding some seaweed, which slipped and in reaching I went over the side. At the time we were close to shore but my Aunt immediately jumped over after me, which meant she was nearly up to her neck in water, while my Dad and Uncle were up the top of the beach roaring with laughing – that is until my Aunt got close to them.

There was no such thing as electric lights, mains water or a sewerage system of any sort. We had paraffin lamps downstairs and candles in the bedrooms. Water came from a big cement tank in the backyard catching the rain from the roof, which was piped through the wall into the kitchen with just enough height above the floor for the water to run by gravity into a bucket. If we had a very dry spell during the summer we would get water in pitchers or buckets from the well in the back lane. The well water could be a bit salty sometimes so we then got it from the public tap down the road. When our tank was nearly empty we drained it off, scrubbed it out and lime washed it. If in between times the water became wormy, a muslin rag was put over the tap and a lump of lime was thrown into the tank, which sorted out the problem.

There was an outside toilet in the backyard and this consisted of a wooden seat with a hole in it, which could be lifted up to allow the bucket to be removed and emptied. The bucket was taken down to the beach and emptied at low water as late as possible in the evening. This was the normal practice in the town houses at that time. This happened well into my boyhood and although people went swimming, fishing and shrimping in the harbour, no one appeared to get ill as a result of it. This makes me sure that all the different substances put into the sewerage systems do far more harm than the raw waste used to, and they are far more dangerous to health.

I was, I believe three years old when we moved into our house, which was a new building rented from the Duchy of Cornwall – at that time there were no freehold houses. We were certainly not a 'well-off' family but my father was self-employed. He and his brother owned a fishing boat together, also a sailing boat each and they used to take visitors out in both sailing boats after tending their crab pots during the summer months. In the winter Dad could always get work, usually around the harbour or in the Steamship Company boats – this was better than the labourer's pay of one pound eighteen shillings per week.

My mother was a dressmaker so she made all our clothes. We had a vegetable garden, which mainly my grandfather looked after. We had our own hens, which meant that we had fresh eggs when they were laying and pickled ones when they were not. There was also plenty of fresh fish and crab with pickled or marinated pilchards in the winter.

During the winter months I used to make an extra shilling or two by delivering telegrams. The farmers used to get telegrams from the flower salesmen, advising them of the prices their flowers had brought on the markets. There were no telephones at that time except for life-saving or government phones. The Post Office was only a few doors away and so the girl on duty in the evenings would bring the telegrams to the door for us boys to deliver on a bike that I had made up from spare parts collected from the dump. The bike was modified as and when better parts were available! The money earned from this job all went into the housekeeping pot and we got a few extra sweets, so everyone scored.

One summer us boys slept in an old First War army tent for a spell to allow Mother to take in visitors. This was good fun until we had a heavy thunderstorm and had to move into the garden hut in the middle of the night!

Family left to right: George, Me, Mum, Dad, Richard, Harry.

12

CHAPTER 2

SCHOOL AND EARLY WORK

I WAS NOT a bad scholar but I hated every moment of it, and seemed to always manage to be in trouble, lots of times with some other boys – usually Guthrie Pender and Melvin Bennett (who were of like spirit and hated school). We would what we called 'go minching', which meant that instead of going into school we would just run off and hide until the others were gone in, then we would go shore hunting, rock jumping (which usually ended with a fall into the sea) or if it was apple season we could go pinching apples at one of the many small orchards. We were always busy as boys; we had lots of games, which cost nothing such as football, cricket, or rounders. As long as we had a ball we were OK, we also used to play a game called 'handy over'. We picked two sides and then one team went one side of an old house or the school and the other team took the ball to the other side. The ball was thrown over the roof shouting, 'Handy', and the other side then tried to catch the ball and if it was caught they shouted 'Over'. The person who caught it would run to try and hit someone from the other side with the ball before he could get to their side of the building. If they managed to score a hit on someone, that person then became one of their side, and so eventually one lot became the winning side. Other games were marbles, hoops, jump back and leap the long mare, in which two sides took part. One lot would bend down in a row up against a wall, and the other side all try to jump on their backs until they are all on top. If the full side managed to get on without the side underneath collapsing then the jumpers won. If any of the jumpers fell off at anytime, then that side had to line up and the others were then the jumpers.

In the winter evenings we would sometimes get up to what we thought was an 'innocent bit of fun'. At the same time we knew that if we were caught or if our parents found out about it, we would be in real trouble and this I suppose made up part of the excitement. One of these tricks was called 'Devil up the pipe'. We would find some old paper or cardboard and stuff it up someone's roof drainpipe – the long ones were the best. We then lit the paper at the bottom and when it really started burning (the pipe acted as a funnel with a terrific draft) it made an awful roaring noise both inside and outside of the house. Another trick was to find two houses with their front doors separated by only a pillar or a column of blocks and we would tie the two door handles together, leaving the rope a little slack. We then knocked at both doors and when they were both pulling hard against each other, we would cut the rope and run to a safe distance where we could not be seen or recognised, to watch the fun.

When I was about eight years old we had a surprise visitor drop in from Canada. This was a small single engine land plane, which after crossing the Atlantic and running short of fuel had landed on Pentle Bay beach at low water. We were used to flying boats or twin floated seaplanes but a plane with wheels was something special – particularly as it had come all the way across the Atlantic. The next day a flying boat came in from Plymouth with fuel for the Canadian visitors – I believe there were two aboard the aircraft for the transatlantic trip. The pilot of the flying boat was Teddy Bureling, a local man. Dad and Uncle Jim were asked to take the petrol from the flying boat up to Tresco, so my brother Harry and myself were allowed to go with them. The pilot let us climb up to look aboard at all the levers, dials and switches, which to us in those days was fascinating. They also gave us a tin, shaped like a travelling trunk with some of their un-wanted, by them but very welcomed by us sandwiches. This tin I still have now, very much worse for the wear but a reminder of a great day for us at the time.

We were very loyal to each other at school and if anyone what we called 'split' on another (meaning told tales to the teacher) or gave what we called 'the game away', that boy would be despised and never trusted again. I remember one occasion when this trust was really tested. We had some outside toilets with leaky roofs, which were basically wooded seats with a hole, and the contents ran down a pipe to the rocks and beach and sea just below. One morning after a bad gale we found that several of the roofing slates had been blown away. One of the gang suggested that if we removed some more they would have to put on a new roof and we could then stand or sit in comfort. The outcome was that when we finished there was no doubt that a new roof was necessary! We were five boys involved, but another boy not of our gang saw what had happened and he told the Headmaster. He knew there were five of us but only knew three names. The Headmaster then had the three questioned as to who the other two were, but after being questioned by everyone including the Police and Town Clerk etc. they could not get these boys to split on us the other two. One of them, the oldest of us was expelled as it was assumed that he was the leader. They were in fact wrong about that, and the authorities never did know who the other two were, much to our relief.

The particular Headmaster of that time was a very bad example having his own favourite pupils according to their parents' bank balance or position. As I have said I was a reasonable scholar at school and in general got on with all the teachers except him. We were a bit of trouble to them at times, but if found out took our punishment without complaint, but I will never forgive this man for ruining my education. At the end of each term a number of the top of the class were sent to the Top Class according to the room available. This particular year there were five places available and I was third from the top of our class and so should have moved to the Top Class, but being quite small the Headmaster decided to take three pupils below me. This made me very mad and from then on I did not have much interest at all, and I must admit I was not the best member of the class when I joined his class at a later date.

I left school at the age of thirteen after a row with the Headmaster. It was because on one particular Friday, which was always test day, two of our gang and myself were accused of copying our maths papers from each other. I can honestly say that as far as I was concerned it was not true. Anyway, he took the three of us out into the annex, made us drop our trousers and gave us a beating on our bare flesh – enough to draw blood. As usual we had agreed that if he beat us badly we would run home, and so when he finished and told us to pull up our trousers we ran straight out the porch door tearing up our test papers as we went. When I got home my mother wanted to know why I had come home from school so soon, so I told her what had happened and she could see I was having a job to sit down. I was made to let her see that he had brought the blood on my backside with the cane, she then washed me and she said, ' You wait until your father knows about this'.

When Dad arrived home from the boat at about six in the evening I was taken straight out to the Doctor, but the Doctor who was a great golfing partner of the Headmaster made the excuse that he would not be able to testify about it because Mum had washed away the actual blood. Anyway, I was told not to go to school first thing but that Dad would take me up when he came later in the morning. So off we went, me being afraid of what Dad would do to the Headmaster. When we got there Dad went to a classroom and asked the teacher (who had grown up with him), 'Where's that B---- B----?' She went to fetch him and as he came into the porch Dad went forward and grabbed hold of his shirt front and drew his fist back. I thought, 'Oh God', but he didn't hit him. He said, 'If you touch that boy once more I will knock your bloody head off your shoulders. If it wasn't for your bloody golfing partner you would be in the court,' and a few more things! He then said, 'Come on boy', and off we went. I was thirteen years old and as we walked home I plucked up enough courage to say, 'What's that mean Dad? Haven't I got to go to school any more? Or can I go to work?' 'You can please yourself,' he said.

I replied that I would rather go to work, and so within a day or two I was working on a farm.

Although the farm work was better than school I really wanted to go on the boats. I did like it better when I learned to drive the pony and then the horse. It was hard work but I didn't mind when I was doing something with the horse or the cob, which was a very high-spirited thing; it was quite a bit of a job at times. When riding bare back he loved to gallop and then stop dead throwing me over his head into the bushes. My wage was seven shillings and six pence per week of six full days from 8 am until 5 pm or quite often a bit later. If we had a very wet week with gales of wind we often worked until dark to get the crop of flowers away and so I would get an extra sixpence or a shilling.

After about two years I managed to get a job in the butchers delivering meat on a bike for a wage of twelve shillings and sixpence. On Tuesday and Friday it was quite busy and I had to do about a five mile round in the morning first thing and then go with Bill the butcher's son who was about ten years older than me, delivering around the rest of the Island in the van.

After a while I used to pester him into letting me drive and if he would not let me, I would get back to the van quickly and then drive off to the next bunch of houses without him. One day I remember I was driving, when out of a by-road without stopping came the dust lorry being driven by the part-time policeman, who was a regular visitor to the slaughter house for a bit of liver or something on killing days. Anyway I was very worried what would happen now, but the next morning the policeman sidled up to me in the butchers and said, 'The next time you are driving that van don't drive so bloody fast'. That was a great relief, as he knew I was under age with no licence.

Bottom Row: Roy Guy, 1st left, Guthrie Pender 3rd left, Roy Jenkins 2nd right, Myself 1st right.
Middle row 1st right: Melvin Bennett.

CHAPTER THREE

THE BEGINNING OF THE WAR

THE NEXT big change was when the war broke out. I was about sixteen and remember I was out in the street with some of the other boys and heard the broadcast through an open window. We were quite excited about it and were also afraid it would not last long enough for us to get involved. Things soon started to change with ration books, blackouts, and soon after the actual act of war.

Just before the outbreak of war in 1937 or 1938 the last of the big German airships, I believe it was the *Lindenburg*, flew in over a wireless station that had been built out on Peninnis headland (very hush-hush), and I remember seeing it fly up to the North of the Islands, turn and then fly back over the station again. I think it was about a week after, it repeated the same trip. At the time it was just a fine thing to see but soon after the outbreak of war we found out why these flights had been made.

I was with a mate of mine in his baker's van going to the garage to put the van away as it was half-day closing for the shops and we were going rabbit shooting, when two twin-engine aircraft flew over and we (who were now members of the Air Training Corps) recognised them as Junkers 88 type. We rushed out to the garage, which was made of galvanized sheets and the next thing down came two bombs. We then ran back to the public toilet entrance where we could watch what was going on. The aircraft would fly towards the wireless station in turn dropping two bombs each on each run, until they used up their load. They did not hit anything but the gorse bushes around it, they also machine gunned along the sea front which was about fifty yards away from where we were watching, and my Dad was moving around behind a telephone pole as they passed, spying at them with his telescope. The bombing of this Direction Finding station went on for more than a week. Every day as regular as clockwork, at I think about twenty-five minutes passed two, the aircraft (sometimes two and other times four) would arrive, and on the last day they managed to set fire to the gorse bushes around the station and so the wood building was burnt to the ground. At that time there was nothing to stop them, and when they were flying around they were so low I remember we could see the man in the cockpit quite easily.

Many people went to the mainland during this time, as they were afraid of a German invasion of the Islands, but most returned as soon as the Direction Finding station was destroyed and the regular bombing stopped.

Soon after this we had one of the best wrecks I can remember, it was a small merchant ship called the *Longships*. My father was coxswain of the lifeboat following on from my grandfather who was coxswain before him, so my brothers and I always knew what was going on. In those days there was no telephone exchange and originally as far as I can remember only five telephones. They consisted of a wooden box about 18 by 9 inches and about 5 inches deep; this was fastened onto two wood slats across the small landing window. It had a voice piece that stuck out the front and could be adjusted up and down and on the right hand side was a handle to wind and ring the bells. There were two bells on the top for incoming calls, in our case the coastguard was one ring, the life-boat Honorary Secretary was two, my Dad was three, and if the coastguard wanted Dad and the Secretary at the same time this was five rings and usually meant a lifeboat call. The bell always woke us up and so we would listen to find out what was happening. On this particular night I heard Dad say, 'No, you mean that the Seven Stones is ashore on the Longships'. The reason being that the Seven Stones was the name of some rocks about eleven miles North East of the Islands and also marked by a lightship anchored there to warn shipping, of course also called the Seven Stones lightship, but the Longships are some rocks off Land's End on which there is also a lighthouse, and so there was a little confusion. How could a lighthouse get wrecked on a lightship? So it was agreed that they should launch the lifeboat and go to the Seven Stones to see what was what, of course there was no wireless on the lifeboat or in the coastguard station at this time.

As boys we then used to watch from our front bedroom windows the lights of the lifeboat as she ran down the slipway, and see her cross the harbour and disappear behind the quay. I remember watching all this and thinking, 'I wish I was old enough to be going out with them.' The next morning soon after getting to work we saw the lifeboat returning with a lot of extra people onboard and so we knew then that there really had been a shipwreck on the Seven Stones Ledges. As soon as the news got around several of the local boats were off to see what they could find, either aboard the ship as she was now abandoned as a total loss, or in the water if she had sunk in the meantime. As luck would have it she stayed broken in half and lying across one of the rocky ledges for about three days and to cap it all the stern cargo hold could be got into, also the amidships cabin and wheelhouse etc. The cherry on the cake however, was that she was carrying a general cargo, and so began one of the most exciting weeks in my time. The boats were going out at daylight and returning with all sorts of things, such as hundreds of towels, sheets, clothing material, table cloths, handkerchiefs, suits, oranges, sacks of potatoes, cases of different kinds of drinks, stockings and loads of other things. It was great fun. At the time there was a café on the quay, the doorway of which was right

S.S. Longships.

opposite the steps where the boats were unloading on to a lorry to be taken up to the custom house store. While they were loading the lorry at one side, at times when he saw his chance the café owner was off loading what he could grab on the other side and taking it in the café. I remember some of the men were returning on the boats with different clothes to the ones they were wearing when they set out and sometimes with two suits and a raincoat on. It was like carnival day every day and all the clotheslines on the Islands were full of washing, plus the gorse bushes were covered in new sheets out to dry. I often say that the first long trouser suit I ever had came off a wreck, which was of course the *Longships*. We had our share of clothing etc. but as young teenagers we also enjoyed the apples, oranges, biscuits, and soft drinks as of course the 'Hard Stuff' in those days was only for men. It did not worry us anyway as all our family were non-drinkers, in fact my Dad never touched any alcohol in his life, neither did Mum, and my eldest brother was the only one out of us four boys that touched any alcohol. This sort of wreck, with no loss of life but a great benefit to the Islands, was very welcome and it helped them survive.

It was on the 27th December 1940 that my mother died, she had been ill for some months before and I think this really made me grow up and take on much more responsibility than I would have done normally. My oldest brother Alfred George had joined the R.A.F. just before the outbreak of war and I think the worry of him being away from home and in the R.A.F., plus the sneak bombing of the Islands and all the air raid warnings because of planes passing over at night on their way to bomb Bristol and other places, was the cause of my mother's early death. She was so worried for us all knowing that soon the rest of us boys would be off, and she was also very scared when the bombers were passing over at night. She would shelter under the stairs with my two younger brothers, Harry and Richard, while Dad who was in the A.R.P. and myself who had joined the Auxiliary Fire Service, reported to the control centre. All of these things led to a stroke. I was with her one evening at our garden where we grew our vegetables and kept the chickens, when she complained of being cold and so I packed up the gardening and headed for home, only two or three hundred yards away. As we went down the hill Mum said, 'Can I catch hold your arm?' so I knew right away there was something really wrong. As we got closer to home the more she leaned on me and I could tell she was really ill, as soon as we arrived Dad sent for the Doctor. Anyway, she had had a stroke and was quite ill for some months, but was recovering and was beginning to get about the house etc. On the Boxing Day evening Harry and I had both gone to a dance but late in the evening Dad came down after us to say that Mum was very ill and we had best come home. She was unconscious and so some time later Harry went to bed and I stayed with Dad by her bedside until later that night she passed away.

This was when I really started growing up. I was very, very close to Mum as I had been born while she was recovering from an appendix operation and at the time was still on the mainland living with her father and family until she was fit enough to return home to Scilly. In those days there was no hospital or anything in Scilly and so one had to be sent over to Penzance on whatever transport was available, steamer, boat, or lifeboat as it was long before the flying days. In my younger days I was very small and very thin so I was often given a bar of chocolate or Mum would try to feed me up in some way. It was about two o'clock in the morning when she died and Dad decided there was no point in waking my two brothers, but kept repeating, 'I don't know how I'm going to tell them,' and I just said, 'Don't worry, I'll tell them'. It was about the hardest thing I have ever had to do, but it was the beginning of really growing up and taking on responsibility.

My Aunt Jane, who was Mum's un-married sister came home to look after us. She had lived with us once before when she herself had been ill and she was still not very strong and so I took over a lot of the chores in my spare time.

The Navy had confiscated our fishing boat the *J.M.L.* (named after my Uncle Jim and my Dad Matt and so standing for Jim and Matt Lethbridge), and as there were many war restrictions on the boats lobster and crayfish fishing was impossible. So, my father had taken a job as skipper to one of the Islands' Steamship Company's launches and he got my Uncle a job as skipper of the *J.M.L.* under the Royal Navy. The irony of it was that my Uncle had quite a bit better wage than my Dad and I got the job as deckhand with my Uncle and my wage went from the butcher's boys 12/6 pence up to three pounds sixteen shillings and nine pence per week, which was also much higher than my father's wage. In those days it was all handed over to run the home and I believe I was allowed the sum of 10/- per week of my own, but was expected to save some of it for anything special I wanted.

Our job in the *J.M.L.* covered all sorts of things, by this time 1940–1941 we now had Royal Navy motor launches stationed in the harbour mainly for searching for the crews of aircraft that had crashed at sea and we acted as a tender to them. There was also a flight of hurricane fighter aircraft here, which were always taking off either for practice, or chasing an enemy bomber. When they returned to land we watched to see if they would do a left hand roll in the aircraft before landing, as this meant they had shot down an enemy aircraft of some sort and was referred to as a victory roll. There were also two R.A.F. rescue boats stationed here, they were quite fast 68 feet long, black with big yellow numbers on the bow and stern and also an R.A.F. red white and blue roundel on the bow, this also had a thin yellow circle around it. I did not then think that one day I would be coxswain of one of these same boats. At that time I only wanted to be a spitfire pilot when I was old enough. There were also mooring buoys in the harbour and in a bay at the opposite side of the Island ready to be used for mooring Sunderland flying boats, as this had now become an emergency landing base, and so another job of ours was to tend on them. I remember one Sunderland that landed here was badly damaged by enemy fighters and she was beached on the town beach. A repair gang of R.A.F. boys came over and she was repaired, we then put her on one of the buoys and set about refuelling her. Towing out a Navy cutter loaded with 10 x 40 gallon drums of 100% octane petrol did this. While we were pumping the fuel up (by hand) my Uncle suggested that as we could only get half the petrol aboard before dark it would be wise to put some on each side to keep the aircraft balanced as the tanks were in the wings. Also, the weather forecast was bad and if she had a list the float on the heavy side could be damaged. Anyway, the crew insisted that we should put it all in the one side and that she would be all right. As they had the final say this was done, but during the night there was a gale and the next morning the Sunderland was sunk and a total loss. She had broken off the float on that side and of course listed over and went to the bottom. We were clear of all blame, but it was a shame especially after so much work had been put in on her.

One of our other jobs was collecting the troops' mail from the off islands. At the time these troops were here practicing landings on beaches etc., several of the local passenger boats were involved in it, locally crewed and under what was called the 'War Department' and at this stage under a real old fashioned Navy ex-Admiral I believe who had returned to service as a Captain. He was quite a disciplinarian in some ways, that is where work was involved, but in other ways loved a bit of game. For instance some of the launch skippers would try to get a day off by saying that the weather was too bad for boat work. His office looked out over the harbour and he would know what it was like and so if he thought otherwise would ring up our Navy phone and say, 'Tell them to get the boat or boats loaded and I will be going with them'. To show the sort of man he was, one morning there was a really fresh North Easterly wind and we were supposed to go to St. Martins for mail in our boat, which was quite a lot smaller than the others. Anyway off we went and after we got out of the shelter of the land I had to start pumping out the water that was coming aboard, otherwise it would get caught up in the fly wheel and thrown over the Magneto and therefore stop one of the engines. I was pumping all the rest of the way, on the way back it was fair wind and so no worries, that is until we were nearing the pier, when we saw Admiral Pilchard as he was known, marching back and forth across the pier end. As soon as we got alongside he turned on my Uncle Jim and really tore him off a strip ending up by saying, 'Lethbridge a man of your experience should have more sense than to go up there on a morning like this'. Uncle Jim was second coxswain of the lifeboat and of course was a fisherman all his life, also had spent several of his early years away in the deep sea merchant ships and so the old Admiral recognised someone who would not easily say, ' It was too dirty,' (as we called it) to do any job we were called on to do.

Before I finish with him I must tell you about one Christmas. He asked all the staff to come for a drink with him in the bar of his hotel 'The Atlantic' between 6.30 pm and 7.00 pm. I personally was not, and never have been a drinker of alcohol but went for my usual lemonade. As the time passed the Admiral plus many of the others were getting very, very happy. I left about half past eight and things were, as you would say really buzzing. The next morning Christmas Day I was on my way to work and as I got nearly to 'The Atlantic' doorway he came out, head down as usual. On seeing me a big grin went over his face and he said, 'Good morning Lethbridge'. But that twinkle in his eye and the grin said an awful lot more both to him and me.

Another one of our jobs was if a mine washed in somewhere we would take the mine disposal chaps to wherever it was so that they could blow it up. Another job which was not very nice at all was that if a body was found or seen on any of the other Islands or rocks, we would have to recover it and bring it back for a military funeral, sometimes Royal Navy sometimes Royal Air Force. I remember one poor chap in particular among others, he was in a really terrible state, had been in the water for a long time and was smelling terrible. Anyway we got the body rolled up in a tarpaulin and in the punt, which we towed back to St. Mary's and put the body in the mortuary and then went home for dinner.

When we returned the engineer Algy Guy turned to Dick Edwards who came with us as an extra hand on this trip and who was a real rough old hard drinking chap and said, 'I couldn't face any bloody dinner today after that one, I took one look and that was enough'. Dick says, 'I didn't even go home, I went to the pub so that was all the dinner I wanted'. Then Algy said, 'What about you Jim?' who replied that he made the attempt but gave it up as a bad job. He then looked at me and said, 'Did you have any dinner boy?' I was then about late sixteen or early seventeen and I felt very guilty replying that I had, he then wanted to know what I had for dinner. So very sheepishly I said that I'd had a pasty for dinner, 'How the devil could you eat a pasty after that?' they said. The two local policemen then came to strip the body of his identity discs or anything like a watch or anything personal at all. When Uncle Jim took them to the mortuary they took one sniff and look and wouldn't go in. Algy and Dick said they weren't going to do it as this was not their job, which was very true and so my Uncle turned to me saying, ' Come on boy, we will have to do it', and so we did. It was a very nasty job. My worst job was after it was all over and the burial had taken place, I had to go in and pick up any uniform, clothing etc. and put it in a sack and return it to the Naval storeroom. I can still remember the feel of wet Hessian sacks on the side of my neck, and the awful smell that went with it, but it was all a good lesson for the future.

Our main job was fishing for the Army and Naval base, there were several hundred soldiers here at that time and after their boat work and general training was completed a company from a different regiment would replace the company. When this happened the local steamship, which was now repainted black and armed against aircraft and submarines was escorted back and forth by two R.M.L.'s and one or sometimes two hurricane fighter aircraft, she also for a while flew a barrage balloon from her foremast. Another of our little jobs at times was to meet the *Scillonian* on her arrival when the balloon which was quite a large thing was then hauled down and transferred to a couple of us on the pier. We then walked up to the old pier where we lashed a net over it for the night. I suppose this was to stop the balloon from putting a strain on the ship's mooring ropes and possibly being a danger to the local and visiting aircraft and flying boats.

This job was under Naval control and yet was with the freedom of doing the actual jobs in our own way with very little interference from anyone. The local Customs and Excise Officer, who had been given a commission as a First Lieutenant in the Navy was our boss. He had been in Scilly for a year or two before the war started, and therefore knew everyone especially the people connected with the sea, which was a big advantage. I spent many hours in Mr. and Mrs. Williams' house as their children John, Iris and Ray were all at school the same time as I was and they helped a lot at the time of my mother's passing. Everyone of course came under old Cap'n Pilchard as he was known and a fine old man he was.

The time was coming for me to try and get into the Air Force. By now I was getting towards 17¾, which was the time when one could officially volunteer for a particular service. Also things had now sorted themselves out at home and I was itching to get flying, I asked Dad about it and he was willing for me to go and so the application was sent off. I was accepted as A1 but had to go for another special flying medical and education test and if all went well one would then sit before a selection board of fairly high ranking officers who questioned you on your life up to then and what you intended for the future. This was to turn out to be one of my great disappointments. I was always quite small for my age and also very thin in fact as a young boy my mother was always insisting that I went to the Doctors for an examination and the Doctor always gave the same report that health wise there was nothing in the world wrong with me except that I had too much energy and that was not a bad thing. Thinking back I believe what really worried Mum was that I had been born while she was recovering from an appendix operation, as I've already said. But to get back to my examinations, I passed all of them with no great trouble and so was then sent before the selection board of officers. After a spell of questions about where I came from, the general way of life there, why I wanted to become a fighter pilot, how long I had been in the Air Training Corps etc. the Air Commodore who was in charge told me that I would be accepted for training as a pilot observer or navigator which were all in the same group. He then said that I should now go to another room where I would be tested for colour blindness and also to have my leg length measurement taken, as this was very important as a pilot. He said, 'When they sit you against the wall to measure your legs I suggest you ease yourself off the wall as I think you may have a job to make the measure, but don't let them see you do it'. I did as he suggested but the sergeant measuring me pushed me back again. Also as I was having my eyes tested for colour blindness, I read several numbers and letters and then came to a couple that seemed to be just a scribble of a line. At that time the medical officer came into the room and asked the sergeant how I was doing and he answered that I seemed to have some trouble as I could not distinguish some of the numbers and could only see twisted lines. The officer then asked me to trace the line with my finger, which I did on two or three of the cards. The officer then turned to the Flight Sergeant and said that it was not I that was colour blind but the sergeant himself. I then returned to the selection board where the Air Commodore told me that I was a little too short in the leg but suggested that as I was under age for calling up I could return home for three months and with some exercise I should make up the leg length. As I had passed all my other examinations I would not have to take them again and would be accepted.

Although I was very disappointed I could not face waiting any longer and so said that I would join the motorboat section. I went to a different room and said that I wanted to volunteer for the motorboat section, the corporal said that there were no more vacancies but I could join as an armourer or as a general duties entrant. This struck me as rather stupid in the middle of a war, so I told him that I would join the Royal Navy instead. As I was going out he called to me to wait as he had now found that there were just two more vacancies, so I told him I would have one of them and that was the start of another change of lifestyle.

CHAPTER FOUR

THE R.A.F.

I RETURNED HOME for a couple of weeks until my papers came through to report to Penarth for kitting out. I remember the train journeys etc. had me really worried as I had never been anywhere past Plymouth, and then it was only once with a troop of Sea Scouts when I was quite young. Never the less after pestering people on the train as to where we had stopped (because all the stations' signs had been removed) I managed to get to Penarth where with others we were kitted out etc. over about ten days and then were sent to Weston-super-Mare for our 'square bashing' as this general training was called. I was very lucky in this as part the way through the training, when we were practicing drill, I managed to stick a bayonet in my hand and was then excused marching etc. for about two weeks. Instead I used to look after the Flight Sergeant's bike for him – he was also a very small man and I think he had a bit of time for me. The only snag was that during the twelve weeks when we were doing any new P.T. exercise or anything he would say, 'Come on Titch, you show them how to do it,' and so I always had to have the first go. This was just like school etc. I was always boxing or fighting someone much bigger than myself.

During the time I was at Weston, we had about four nights of heavy air raids, the first in the area. On the first night I was standing on guard in the Headquarters doorway, right opposite the pier with a rifle and five rounds of ammunition which was passed onto the next guard on relief, scared stiff, but not able to leave. On the second night when we saw fires and the explosions, two or three of the chaps in our room suggested that we went to see if we could help. This was the first of many times that I was to break the rules, but always managed to get away with it. We went into the middle of town arriving at one street, which was burning from end to end except for two buildings in the middle. On one side two or three of the Firemen with portable fire pumps were trying to save these, and after asking if we could help we were told to go inside these buildings and go up through the storeys to see if the fire was creeping through. When we returned there was no sign of the firemen, so as the pump was still there and I had been in the Auxiliary Fire Service at home we started it up and had a go until the petrol ran out. We then went further up the burning road and met an old chap outside a small shop that was well alight and he begged us to help him as he was a shoemaker and his machine was just inside the lower room but it was far too heavy for him to move. He said that if we could get it out for him he would not care about the shop as he felt that as long as he had his machine he wouldn't have to worry he would always be able to earn his living. We managed to get it out on to the pavement and the poor old chap was so grateful hugging and thanking us that we felt really embarrassed but he seemed to be so happy amongst all this trouble. During these raids there were many casualties and deaths and after that night we all had to report for duties at Headquarters when there was a raid.

After passing out drill in which our flight was top group we all split up and went our different ways, as the Marine section was a small part of the Air Force and at that time was for volunteers, I found myself posted to Bridlington in Yorkshire on my own. On arrival I reported to the Headquarters, which was a hotel that had been taken over by the R.A.F. after the outbreak of war. I felt quite at home here as we were about four or five to a room, with mess room, sitting room, and cookhouse etc., but most of all there were plenty of different types of Royal Air Force boats and loads of fishing boats and fishermen around the harbour. We got on very well with the locals especially the fishermen, and I remember on different occasions as we were going to our pier office on night duty, we would meet some of the fishermen coming up the pier from their boats and quite often we would be told to look inside the wheelhouse, which meant that there was a cod there for our supper. The reason for this was that our fitter (Engineer) was like myself, from a fishing family at Whitby just up the coast and so knew all about the fishing boats engines etc., and I also had worked in an engineer's workshop. At times we had also been very interested and spent some time with the lifeboat engineer who owned the workshop and when one of the local boats had some problem, usually a Dynamo, or water pump, or electrical they would ask Ted our fitter if he would have a look at it and so as we were only on stand by Air Sea Rescue duty it was no problem to lend a hand. We were alongside the same pier as the fishing boat so Ted would usually manage to fix it and I would be his labourer. Sometimes one of the fishing boats would be late returning as they were only allowed at sea from daylight when we opened the harbour boom to let them out and return before dark. If one was late sometimes the lifeboat coxswain would ask if we could go and have a look for the missing boat because our boats were a lot faster than the lifeboat and so would have more chance in daylight as no lights were shown in wartime. The old Cox used to come with us as he knew the fishing grounds and where they were likely to be. It all used to end up O.K. maybe a little engine trouble or a tow in or trouble with their fishing gear and we would meet them on their way home. This sort of thing kept us as we used to say, well in with the locals. As a matter of interest I was given a great compliment by one of the boat skippers who asked me if I would like to come back after the war and join his crew he said, 'There is always a job here for you if you want it'. I know that he really meant it – I had already learnt that the Yorkshire fishermen are very blunt and never say anything they don't mean, just as they used to be at home. I could tell many stories of my time at Bridlington which I enjoyed very much but I must skip on.

A month or two later we had a visit of what was termed as a travelling trade test board. This meant a Warrant Officer inspector arrived to test us six or seven blokes who were classed as untrained because we had not been to the R.A.F. sea school. Because we had already been working on the boats, we could take the test in boat work, Morse code, semaphore, engine medics and what have you, to see if we were fit to become motorboat crew A.C.2 (Aircraftman 2nd class) instead of untrained personnel. I remember this Warrant Officer after some of the other tests, giving us all a short piece of rope saying that we were to do an eye splice, then a back splice and finally a short splice. This was no problem for me as I had done hundreds over the years. I saw him watching me and when I started to join the two ends he came over and took it out of my hand saying, ' You have no need to bother with that. Where do you come from?' When I answered, 'The Isles of Scilly, Sir', 'Oh that explains it,' says he 'Now go down to the dinghy and row off to that buoy, and then scull back'. I jumped into the dinghy but after about half a dozen strokes he told me, 'That's enough, now scull back.' All these things I had been able to do and had been doing since I was a boy at school, and so I passed out above the average, and was now an Aircraftman 1st class. I was taken off the dog's body job I had been doing and was lucky enough to get assigned to a variety of jobs including target towing, and armour boat work in which the aircraft involved were usually Halifaxes and Lancasters. I was also appointed as dinghy driver, which meant that I was in charge of my own boat. This was an 18 foot open boat with an 8.28 four cylinders Power Meadows engine and normal full speed of 18 knots, but if handled right could come to a stop in just about it's own length. This was achieved with one movement by passing down the little throttle lever, the bow of the boat then dropped and the stern lifted by the following wave, at this point the gear lever was put into reverse and the throttle lever lifted until the boat was stopped.

This action once saved a Seaplane tender running over my Sgt. Coxswain at the time. On the spring tides the duty night crew had to take what boats were required for stand by flying duties (safety boats) out to the mooring buoys outside the harbour to make sure they were afloat when needed and so Dutchie as he was nicknamed (his real surname being Holland) called me early in the morning saying, 'Don't wake the others, Titch, (as I was always known) you and I can manage. I will take two of the boats tied together, and you take the other one and the dinghy. Drop your boat onto the buoy and then come over to give me a hand with the other two.' All was going well; off I went and had just moored my Seaplane tender up when I heard someone calling out for help. As it was just breaking daylight I could not see his boat from where I was, but knew the direction anyway. I jumped into the motor dinghy, and I headed flat out to where I thought he would be. Sure enough he was right ahead in the water but there also was a Seaplane tender heading straight for him, at a speed of about three or four knots. I had visions of her going right over him and the propellers chewing him to pieces, but I did not know if I would have time to push her off course with the dinghy or should I try to grab him first. Anyway I went for him and as I have already said stopped her right alongside and as the bow dropped he grabbed hold of it and the forward movement dragged him with it. The Seaplane tender then hit the dinghy right amidships about five or six feet from him, this was a great fright at the time but as I was helping to drag him onboard I noticed one of his white sea boot stockings had nearly come off and so it looked as if one of his legs was the normal length and the other was at least twice the size. This made me roar with laughter but poor old Dutchie did not think it funny as the other boat was still going around in circles with no one aboard. We soon caught up with her and all was well once more.

There was one other time we were very much in trouble. We were at the time, the duty Air Sea Rescue crew one night and received a crash call from Air Ministry of a Halifax having crashed, I think it was about 20 miles off Flamborough Head. Off we go flat out, as we were going out along the coast Dutchie told me to get the recognition signals of the day from our wireless operator in case the shore batteries challenged us on asking for them. The W/O says 'Oh my goodness (or something like that) I have left them in the wireless cabin'. This was a bit of a snag but Dutchie says, 'What do you think about turning all our lights on Titch and hope they will know what is going on'. We felt that we couldn't return and so we switched on at first the navigation lights and then we decided we would give them a better chance by putting on our cabin lights as well and crossed everything, especially our legs and proceeded flat out. As we were nearing Flamborough it struck me that with the wind in that particular direction there could be some minesweepers anchored on the other side in the shelter. This was worse than the shore batteries as they would have a much closer shot and many more guns. Dutchie decided we should wait and see if they were there, sure enough as we rounded the head there were five minesweepers. Another snag was that the German E boats quite often operated in this area attacking coastal convoys, but as we were already in sight of the minesweepers we just merrily sailed right passed them with all lights shining brightly. After searching on the position for sometime, we met the Filey lifeboat and on first sight thought their yellow oil-skins were the yellow dinghies but they informed us that they were on their way home and had been told that if they met us to tell us also to return as they were unable to contact us. On going in the cabin to tell the wireless operator to let base know we were returning, we found that the wireless set was in perfect order but the wireless operator was in a very sorry state and did not seem to have heard the recall and did not seem to care much but just wanted to die, poor chap. He was a lovely great chap and full of fun but not cut out for bouncing around in a boat and we were doing quite a bit of that.

After a few months I was again promoted to Leading Aircraftman (L.A.C.) and a while after this our own warrant officer asked me if I would like to go on a coxswain's course and so off I went to Stranraer and on to Coreswall camp. This was a camp of Nissen huts in woods at the end of Loch Ryan. It was a camp set up for American soldiers but they soon decided they didn't want it and so the R.A.F. decided it was just the place for us. I must admit that as a training base it was good because it was on the bank of a long well sheltered loch, but with immediate access to the open sea and just the job for navigation exercise over to Belfast or Girvan Ayr or anywhere one wanted to go. The camp itself was a miserable affair. We were sixteen to a hut; there was a diesel stove but only enough fuel for about two evenings a week and it was freezing cold in winter. The showers and washroom meant a tramp of about between one or perhaps three or four hundred yards (depending on which hut one was in) only clad in underpants or P.T. shorts and P.T. vest. So to come out of having a shower and then tramp back to the hut was not really enjoyable. There was nowhere to go as Stranraer was about six miles away and the buses were few and far between and if I remember one night a week they finished running in the early evening. This was another advantage as a training base because it meant that most of us spent the evenings swatting up for the exams and just went to the N.A.F.F.I. hut for a mug of tea and a bun.

The food was really awful, I had been used to good food, as both my Mother and my Aunt who had come to live with us were the best of cooks, so I was far from happy with this. Many times I tipped it in the swill bin and waited for the N.A.F.F.I. to open. I remember one time we were in the mess room and the orderly officer and the orderly sergeant came in as usual and asked if there were any complaints. A boy on the next table spoke up and said, 'Yes Sir'. When asked what was wrong he mentioned different things and ended by saying that the food was not fit for a dog. At this, the officer turned to the sergeant, and told him to go outside and bring in one of the dogs that were always around the cookhouse. When the sergeant returned with the dog the chap's plate was put on the floor for the dog but he just looked and sniffed at it and then went out of the door. With that the officer turned to the boy and told him he was a very lucky man because if the dog had eaten any of it then this boy would have been put on a charge. As the dog had refused it, he would take the complaints to the cookhouse. It didn't make any difference but it was nice to know that the chap had at least had his say without punishment and if the dog could talk I reckon he would have said that he was already full up!

After about twelve weeks training in just about every subject in the Royal Air Force manual, including boat work, navigation, engineering, laying moorings, tending on and refuelling and loading flying boats with depth charges etc. we did our exams and I was again lucky enough to get 87%, with a pass mark of 75%. I was well away, I then returned to Bridlington as a 2nd class coxswain and was given a boat for which I had to sign the inventory for the boat and all the equipment listed.

For a period then I was very happy and had some good chaps with me as crew. Most of them like myself hated parades or inspections, but we were perfectly happy to be out in the boat and did not care how many hours we did. We managed to get out of many of these parades and kit inspections by getting ourselves picked to do any unexpected boat work. Smithy was a 'beaut'; I can't remember him ever getting really annoyed with anyone or anything. On maintenance days when our work was finished, Smithy hated to have to hang around doing nothing, especially if it meant it interfered with our expected time off. He was always happy aboard the boat, especially at sea, and never complained about extra duties as long as it was boat work. I remember one time we were just the stand by boat and bored to tears so Smithy came to me to ask if it was O.K. for him to slip off to the pictures not far away. I just reminded him of our understanding, which meant that as far as I was concerned he had gone to the boat repair shed at the top of the pier to get something. 'O.K.' he said, 'Don't worry, I'll carry the can'. This meant he would take the blame saying he had gone without my permission; otherwise I would be in trouble and certainly be stripped of my corporal's stripes. Just after he had left, the W/O was coming down the pier on his bike. I thought, 'Oh God there must be something turned up', and sure enough he says, 'There's a request for a stand-by flying boat at Skipsea Range right away, so get going. Is your crew all there?' Before I could answer he asked, 'Where's Smith?' because he was not in sight and the W/O knew what to expect. At that moment Smithy arrived on someone's bike. 'Where have you been Smith?' says the W/O. With the innocence of an angel Smithy replies, 'Up to the shed Sir'. The W/O just looked at him and says, 'Smith you are the biggest bloody scrounger on this station, and there is not a thing I can do about it', meaning he could never catch him out. Also Smithy used to get a nice cod or something and take it up to the W/O's wife up town, and so that was his excuse if he was caught. I must say these things only happened very rarely and only when we were on a day-off or maintenance day.

I was very lucky with my crews, another pair was Kelly and Freddy, and these were known as the terrible twins. One time we had to take a crewmember back to his steam-fishing drifter that belonged to the Air Force and was used for buoy maintenance around the coast. She was moored outside the harbour and as it was quite a fresh wind she was rolling quite heavily. Kelly managed to get his foot between us and the drifter, breaking his ankle quite badly and he was very concerned to let it be known that it was his own stupid fault as he called it. After a week or two in hospital the great aircrew 'Kelly' returned on crutches and on rest. He was of course able to go to the shows, pubs, or dances and sit or stand around being the centre of attention for the girls, telling them how he was shot up in his Halifax over Berlin and of course then it was free beer etc. for many weeks to come. We were fascinated to listen in on some of his stories, knowing what really happened but enjoying the way he was getting all the sympathy.

These boys and many more were real good mates and although always ready for a bit of fun or cheating the system among ourselves, they were as honest as the day. As I have said I have never been a drinker of any alcohol neither was Dad or two of my three brothers and therefore I usually had a bob or two in my pocket and so was always helping out with a small loan from payday to payday as we were paid every 2nd Friday. By the beginning of the second week regularly Kelly, Fred, and Smithy were broke and so it was ten bob for the next week but on payday it was, 'Here's your ten bob Titch and here's ten or five bob for you to save for me, and don't let me have it until a certain day.' Somehow though, on the second week we were always back to square one. When I was posted from Bridlington it was without warning and I was leaving soon after dinner time but as soon as these boys knew they made sure to borrow from someone else, without any approach from me and repay their loans and there were five of them on that particular day all owing five or ten bob but I left with every penny repaid and a great lot of goodwill between us all.

Before I leave Bridlington I must tell of our armoured boat trips. The boats were much like a seaplane tender – quite fast, I would say about 25–30 knots without the armour we once tried one and it achieved 35 knots. The armour plating only covered the engine and steering compartment and was about one foot high over the engines. It was the same height on each side of the steering position but rising in a curve to allow the coxswain to sit in his seat but with no standing room. The bulkheads fore and aft, of the steering position, both contained a small armoured glass window about 1 foot wide and four inches deep just enough for the cox to see his way around. We had to crawl in, the cox first and then the wireless op and finally the deckhand, these sat one each side of the coxswain's feet. The entrance was a watertight armour door shut by a lever and six dog clips. It was a big joke to us to say that we would never get out of here if we were hit. The bombs used were practice bombs but there was a very big dent in one of the boat's armour plate, which was half to five eighths of an inch thick and weighing I think 15 hundred weight. The aircraft were only allowed to drop 2 bombs at one time. Quite often I would be able to guess how close they would be when they were about half way down and one of these days I told the boys, 'This is going to be really close.' There was a big bang, lots of smoke and a crash as it hit, it went down through the foredeck, the batteries (big ones), then 18 inches or more Onozote (which was sheets of a light floatable material) and then out through the bottom. I reckon we were all outside before it got through the decking. There were big wood plugs in case this happened but they were nowhere near big enough. I thought that if I used my uniform coat and the plugs I could stop the worst of it and also get myself a new uniform because of the acid etc. This is what I did and of course had informed base that we were taking in water fast and did not know if the boat was going to sink or capsize. They sent a tender out at full speed and when she arrived they went past us close by at full speed to turn and take us in tow but we were running from one side of the deck to the other to try and stop her from capsizing and were not amused while they thought it a great joke. The biggest joke was that when or if the boat capsized the armour plate was supposed to just fall off whereby the Onozote would keep her afloat. After it was towed back and half full of water taken straight up the slipway, it took the shipwrights 2 days to get the armour plating off. Never mind it was all good fun and we did get 3d. a day extra for armour boat work.

I was very lucky on one occasion I was the duty cox and with my crew we slept in the pier office, which was a stone tower. We had a civilian night watchman who came on duty at about 8–9 o'clock in the evening until 7 in the morning; he looked after the boats in the harbour while we slept in case we were called upon to go to sea. On the night watchman waking me to say he was going off duty I said, 'Have you noted it in the log book?' 'Yes,' he said, 'Everything in order and signed it'. Most of the coxswains used to wait until just before the day crews arrived but I always got up and walked up the harbour to check the mooring lines for myself. When I got to the top of the harbour there was one of the armour boats high and dry upside down on the slipway. I went straight back and noted it and the time in the logbook and got two of the boys to witness it. Then as soon as the W/O's office opened I rang him and reported. If I had not got out of bed and taken this action I would have been blamed for it but because of the state of tide etc. after reporting it neither the C/O or the W/O held me in anyway responsible – in fact I think they were quite pleased that I had saved a lot of trouble trying to sort out who was responsible for it.

On another occasion I was also very lucky, as duty coxswain we had a phone call from group H.Q. saying that an Air Sea Rescue craft was returning from a search and was somewhere in Bridlington Bay running out of fuel. We were to meet it and tow it in. I did question them if they knew how big an area Bridlington Bay was – it is many miles long and wide and also informed them that it was thick fog and of course dark. We had no radar or anything, just a watch and a compass but agreed to try, thinking it was an impossible job and that we would be lucky to find the harbour again ourselves under these conditions and with no charts either. I decided that we would firstly do a triangle run out to Flamborough Head then down across the bay to Skipsea Range where if we were lucky we would find the bombing and firing targets and so know the course back to the harbour. As luck would have it after about a third of this was completed we ran straight into the High Speed Launch and so took her back to the mooring buoys. The coincidence was that as we went alongside the other coxswain opened his wheelhouse window and shouts, 'What are you doing out on a night like this Titch?' (as a joke). He was an old mate of mine that had been posted away and was now at Grimsby.

Not long after the harbour affair the W/O stopped me on the pier one day and asked me if I would like to go on a first class coxswain's course to which I agreed that I would be very pleased to. He then told me that he was breaking the rules to send me as there was a time limit between these courses and I was only about half way through, but he told me that he was very sure that I would pass and he was willing to take the chance of sending me and so off I was posted to Scotland soon after.

The camp had not changed but on arrival I met one of my best old mates, Pat, who was now on his first coxswain's course and Dutchie who was now a Pilot Officer on his skipper's course, but the same old Dutchie to me. Pat was older than I and had been in the service quite a while longer but although his trade had been a glass blower, as a boat handler one would think he had been brought up in boats like myself. On top of that he was quite well educated I would think, because when it came to anything concerning figures or trigonometry he was brilliant and this of course also made him brilliant at navigation.

Easter weekend came while we were there and Pat suggested that because Ted Heath and his dance band were playing in Ayr that weekend we ought to go. So we got a weekend pass and Pat who was a great boy for the girls, chatted up the local bus conductress whom we both often saw when going into Stranraer. She agreed that if we took the chance we could get a free ride except for the last stop when she would take our money and issue us with a ticket, or if the inspector came aboard she would have to give us a ticket for that part of the journey. We arrived in Ayr with no snags and set off to try and find somewhere to sleep for a couple of nights. Because it was Easter weekend it was hopeless, and when it came time for the dance Pat decided the best thing was to at least go to the dance and hope to meet someone who would take pity on us. All through the dance we tried with no luck whatsoever and ended up on the street, we then as a last resort went to the police station and asked if we could sleep in one of the cells. This was also refused, we then tried the bus station but the old night watchman when asked if we could sleep in one of the buses refused and told us to get out. On leaving, just outside the gate we decided that as his hut had a high window we could bend right down and creep under it and so that was what we did. We made for the nearest bus but was disappointed to find that it had wood slat seats and after trying a few more which were all the same we went up to the top deck and tried to get off to sleep. By now it must have been about 1.30 in the morning, there was a strong wind, it was drafty, freezing cold, and the seats were as uncomfortable as anything could be. At about 5.30 in the morning Pat calls to me asking if I was awake, I replied that I was still trying to get to sleep, and he then came out with the classic remark, saying, 'God I wish you knew how cold I am'. This seemed brilliant seeing as I was on the next seat, we then decided to creep out of the bus station and walked around until we found a wash and brush up place. This was locked up over night, but over the top of the glass panelled door was a narrow window and by standing on Pat's shoulders I found it would open. In trying to get through I put my knee against the glass panel of the door and there was an awful noise as the panel cracked, but luckily it did not fall out. I then opened the door and after a quick strip wash in lovely warm water we had pulled on our clothes and were just going to open the door when we heard someone outside. It was the cleaner. As he opened the door I put my hand on the glass to stop it from falling out, and then as this poor old chap stood there looking at us for a second and then at the door which he had just unlocked Pat shoved a shilling in his hand and we were gone. The next night we spent sleeping in an old lady's sitting room, who also gave us some breakfast and did not want us to pay her for any of it, because she said that she was a widow with a son in the Merchant Navy and she hoped someone somewhere may also help him if he needed it. We of course did leave her some money and tried to let her know how grateful we were. We also again managed to get a cheap trip back on the bus with our favourite bus conductress.

When it came to my exam I was doing fine until I was taking my oral exam - the noted old squadron leader that was in charge of the school had come back out of retirement and walked into the room. After a while he asked the examiner how I was getting on, to which he replied by saying that I was doing quite well, he then turned to me asking me if I thought that the course would help me. I, like a fool answered, 'Yes Sir, it will come in very handy after the war'. At this he blew his top and remarked that this motorboat crew course was not to help me after the war. The examiner then interrupted saying that I was not on a crew's course but a coxswain's course. This did not help his blood pressure at all and he wanted to know how old I was and how long I had been in the R.A.F. I replied that I was 19 years old and had been in the Air Force about 18 months. '18 months', he repeated, 'I was seven years before I was a 2nd class coxswain.' At this the instructor interrupted again saying, 'No Sir, he is not on a 2nd coxswain's course but is already a 2nd class coxswain and is on his 1st class coxswain's course'. I really can't remember the rest of this discussion he was so surprised and annoyed that a young shrimp like me should be in this position that I knew then my chances were going out the window fast. I was now determined to try harder than ever to prove to the likes of him that I could do this job possibly a lot better than an old fool like him. This sort of work had been my life, even as a school boy and the little I had learned of navigation from my A.T.C. days was from the R.A.F's own book and so this had given me at least a little advantage. The navigation side of the exams were the next and last part of the total examination. My mate had shown me a very simple, quick and foolproof way of dealing with the type of problems, which I was likely to get in the exam. It concerned something like – what was a position from horizontal angles and bearings? Anyway, as expected there was one of these among the five questions on the exam paper for which we were allowed 2 hours. As this was very easy for me to do now I used Pat's way of dealing with it and had more time to complete and check my paper with which I felt quite confident. The day after I was called to report to the exam boardroom, this I did and found the same examiner, also the same old Squadron leader, there was my chart and work paper laid on the desk in front of them. The Squadron Leader then asked me how I had done this problem; I replied by asking him, ' Is it right Sir?' 'Oh well, yes it's right, but how did you do it? And where are the figures involved'. I pointed to the, I think, three lots of figures and said, 'That is all you need sir'. He was getting more and more worked up and said, 'Show us how it works'. I then told them that my mate had shown me how to do it and proved to them that it was a much quicker and safer way of dealing with these problems. I also showed them how easy and foolproof it was. Instead of using this method in the future (which he agreed was right) he just took my paper and crossed off the whole lot saying, 'In future you do it our way'. By this it meant that I had been robbed of 15 points, which also meant that I now was left with only 74% when the pass rate was 75%. If that old fool had allowed me my 15 marks or even let me do the problem over again in the Air Force way I would have passed quite easily. That was typical of the service style and so I was on my way, but when I got my posting it was for Falmouth, which was the parent station for Newlyn. As Newlyn was short of 2nd coxswains the next day I was off to Newlyn.

I was immediately appointed to High Speed Launch 2552 as her 2nd Coxswain. This was one of the very boats that I had admired when they had arrived in Scilly, when I was still a civilian working under naval control. I was delighted, and I did not know just how lucky I was. The skipper a Flight Lieutenant Wheeler was an ex-Merchant Navy Officer. A great gentleman, a great skipper and a very popular man with the crew. The first cox, Johnny Johnston or Johnson was also the salt of the earth and we were all a very happy crowd and also proud of our boat. Only once did Mr. Wheeler ever attempt to suggest that something needed doing while I was on that boat. One morning he came aboard, at the time I was watching him from the little bridge and so went aft to say, 'Good morning'. He then hesitantly said he had just looked down the tiller flat, the hatch of which was open, (I had seen him do this) and he carried on, 'I was wondering if we could give it a bit of a clean up?' I just grinned and said, 'Well Sir that is why the hatch is open, we have washed it down and are waiting for it to dry so that we can re-paint it.' He was really annoyed with himself and slapped the side of his leg saying, 'I'm sorry Coxswain, I should have bloody well known better'.

When we were duty boat he would sometimes come over to the fo'c'sle door, which was always open. He would then tap the door and ask if he may come in and join the card schools. I did not play cards much but when the boys were playing I would use one of their canvas bunks to lie on, usually to read a book. One evening I was doing just that and as I glanced out through the passage up to the sick bay, where Johnny and I slept, I saw flames on the side of the boat just where the shore lighting plug came aboard. For just a second it did not register and I quietly said, 'There's a fire out there,' and went to look back at my book, then suddenly realizing what I had said, there was a sudden rush. I managed to get out first grabbing an extinguisher as I went, as I went to strike it the fitter who was right behind me, knocked it out of my hand and set off the one he was holding. We soon had the fire out, and he had probably saved me from at least a very bad electric shock, because I had grabbed the wrong type of extinguisher. A fire on our type of boat was really dangerous because our engines ran on 87% octane petrol.

One day when we were stand-by boat, I had to go up the pier and look after the W/O's office. He was a good sort and I got on fine with him. He was going to Falmouth for the afternoon to arrange stores, which was normal, and he told me that the three trainees were painting and cleaning up the base huts, so to keep an eye on them. When it came to teatime, up they came to the office and asked if they could stay there with me while they had their break. As I was sat in the W/O's chair with my feet up on his desk and the three boys sat around all drinking mugs of tea, in comes a strange Squadron Leader. He nearly had a fit and managed to say, 'Who is in charge here corporal?' As I was the only one with the stripes on his arm I thought, 'You silly sod, who do you think is in charge,' and said, 'I am Sir'. To which he replied, 'Well what is going on here?' My brain was working like a jet engine and I told him that these airmen had just finished cleaning the base huts and wanted to know what to do next, so I had told them, 'We can discuss that while you have your break to save time'. This answer floored him and he said, 'Well there is no need to sit there with your feet on the W/O's desk while doing so', and off he went. When the W/O came back, he asked me if everything was O.K. 'Yes Sir fine.' says I. 'O.K. get back to your boat', and I was gone like a shot. I had no sooner got aboard when the shore phone rang. 'Come up to my office right away', I am told. When I got there he told me that the inspector of Air Sea Rescue for the South coast had given the C/O a rocket and he had then passed it onto the W/O, who was passing it onto me with extras. I was to be stripped of my rank and God knows what. I was just looking at him half smiling to myself when he ran out of words, he then says, 'I don't think you care Lethbridge'. I replied, 'Not very much Sir'. He looked at me in exasperation saying, 'Oh get back to the bloody boat,' and that was the last I heard of it.

One morning the skipper comes aboard and tells me that a 24 foot marine tender has arrived on the base and it is to go over to St. Mary's for the naval base to tend on the Sunderlands as they were using St. Mary's as an emergency landing base more often now. The skipper also asked me how I felt about him and me steaming it over on our day off. I was all for it and so he went up to see our C/O to suggest it to him, but it wasn't long before he returned looking disappointed telling me that the C/O would not allow it. He said, 'You have to go up to the office now because you have to go over with it.' I found that I had to get it into the water by the harbour crane and get my kit packed, as a fitter and myself were to run it over to Penzance in the morning and load it onto the *Scillonian*. We would then stay in Scilly for two weeks with the tender or until the Navy were happy. After two weeks Mr. Williams who was the assistant Resident Naval Officer agreed for the fitter to return but stated that he wanted me to stay for another two weeks. I then returned on the steamer to Penzance and reported into the base around about 1pm and found that our boat was day off and so I went to my billet.

My billet was at the top of Paul Hill, quite a long steep hill it was. The old couple I was billeted with were a lovely couple called Mr. and Mrs. Evans and as I was the only one there I was really spoilt. We lived aboard when on duty and stand-by boat, but when on 2 hour or 4 hour boat we lived in our billets.

The next morning I was back aboard and I found that Mr. Wheeler had been posted and we had a new skipper. I could tell that I wasn't going to see eye to eye with this man and luckily I found that I was to take over as 1st coxswain on 2556 while their coxswain was on leave.

The first trip out the skipper started conning the boat from the bridge, where as Mr. Wheeler had always left the coxswain to handle the boat in and

H.S.L. 2556.

out of harbour etc., but at sea gave the course to steer etc. I did not like this conning business and so decided to put a stop to it right away. Where as his old cox would answer his orders and then do what he thought was necessary, I decided to follow his orders exactly. As we returned to Newlyn after going through the entrance the skipper who was a Dutchman, Mr. Senator (a real nice chap but a little excitable) says, 'Hard to starboard Coxswain'. I repeated the order and unlike his old coxswain went hard to starboard. We were now heading straight for the middle of a Navy R.M.L. (I would not have allowed us to hit it, but he didn't know that) and so there was a big panic of, 'Full astern Coxswain,' and again from me, 'Full astern Sir.' We were now tearing across the harbour flat out, 'Full ahead Coxswain,' and, ' Full ahead Sir,' then, 'Stop engines, all right Coxswain take her in.' 'Right Sir, take her in.' I made sure that we made a perfect job and stopped bow out, bow to bow exactly level, and so close one could just step onto the other boat without even touching the fenders. The captain of that boat, 2554, had heard the noise of racing engines and got to his bridge just in time to see us coming alongside and after we berthed he looks over to Mr. Senator saying, 'That was a lovely board Senator, a nice job.' To which he replied, 'Thank you Baylon, thank-you.' So he was happy and did not bother to interfere any more, which was what I had intended.

Another time while I was Mr. Senator's coxswain the base was warned that there was evidence of a German spy working around the South Coast area. We were told to be on our guard when acting as duty boat during the night. Although I had no need to take a watch, I always did and so it turned out that during my twelve to two watch I was up on the bridge looking around, when at about 1.45 am I saw someone creeping down the pier and then down the ladder on to the boats. Being the duty boat we were on the outside and so he had to cross over the standby boat before boarding us. I had already recognised his movements as those of the skipper, so I allowed him to board. As he went down the companion stairway I nipped smartly from the bridge to the top of the stairway leading down into the hull behind him and shouted, 'Halt! Where in the hell do you think you're going?' He nearly fell the rest of the way saying, 'Stop, stop, it's only me, Mr. Senator.' I, of course, was 'very surprised' and apologised with, 'I'm very sorry Sir, I didn't realise it was you.' I told him that I had seen him creeping along and getting aboard so he says, 'Well, why didn't you stop me before I got aboard?' I was ready for this and replied that if I had shouted he would have got away but I had now trapped him on the stairs between the crew below and myself above him. He was very impressed and patted me on the shoulder saying, 'Great thinking, well done Coxswain.' Off he went a very happy man, I expect to tell his fellow officers about the very efficient crew he had.

Soon after I got back to my own boat, I was again told that I was to go back to Scilly to run the tender and the stand-by flying work. I made sure to ask the C/O to make it clear who was my actual boss – was it the Navy or the Air Force Officers? I was told that as far as I was concerned I had been lent to the Navy until further orders and the R.N.O. was my boss so I would take orders only from him. I did this because I could see trouble ahead, and sure enough one day I had a run in with the new skipper of 2552 whom I really did not like at all, and in my opinion was not very good at all. In fact on one occasion, on a foggy morning the R.N.O. rang and asked me if I would lead this man out of the harbour until he was clear to set course for Newlyn. This I did but no sooner had I got back than he was back as well. The coxswain, Johnny, was cheesed off altogether with him and told me that as soon as I had left them, he had turned right around and keeping me just in sight followed me back!

Anyway, one day I was on my way out to land a Sunderland flying boat and this chap was standing on the stern of his boat waiting for me to pick him up, but I just waved no and carried on. When I returned to the pier he was there and again I was going to be charged, stripped and whatever, but I just told him the R.N.O. was my boss and he must take it up with him. This really sent him in a rage, ending by saying, 'You had better never let this happen again.' So I ignored him, pushed the engine into gear and shoved off. I knew what either of the R.N.O.'s would have said if he went and reported me, so I was not even worried by it. Like fate about two days afterwards the same thing happened and I passed quite close and again just shook my head and waved no. I could see he was flaming mad but I ignored it.

Not very long after this I received an overseas posting and at the same time I had to go to Plymouth to give evidence about a flying boat that I tried to talk down in thick fog early one morning. The flying boat had been to Mount

Batten and Pembroke Dock which were both fog bound and now he was out of fuel and had to land. I talked him right around from North West of the Islands by sound and when he was East of me I got him to turn West and come down. He did a fantastic job and although I could not see him until after he passed right over the top of the boat and I knew I was in the centre of the landing area, I told him he was fine and to keep coming down. He then saw some rocks to starboard and I told him, 'That's O.K. you will be O.K.', but he did not like it and decided to go clear of the Islands and try to land. In doing so he knocked off a float, and one of the R.M.L.'s took him in tow, but she sank. There was no fault on the Pilot but it was normal procedure to have a court marshal. While I was giving evidence in front of a board of, I believe, an Air Commodore, two Group Captains, and a Wing Commander, I was asked a few questions and then the Commodore asked me how long it took me to get from my billet to getting the boat away. To this I said, 'About ten minutes'. The Wing Commander trying to show off says that 'that's silly and impossible', and that I could not possibly dress and get out of the house in three minutes. That really made my blood boil, so I forgot where I was and told him, 'Look I am billeted at home, and after Dad called me, I just pulled on my trousers, (as I was sleeping in my shirt) which were on the end of the bed, I then grabbed my tunic which was also there, the tunic I pulled on while I was going downstairs where my sea boots and stockings were waiting in the kitchen and so I slipped into those and straight out the door'. The boat was only a short distance from the house and the pier and so all of this was easily possible for me. After this outburst I realised what I had done and thought, 'Oh my God, now look out.' When I looked at the Air Commodore he was grinning at me and he nodded his head saying, 'Yes and I expect you could'. End of questions and one sick looking Wing Commander. The Commodore then turned to me saying, 'You are Cpl. Lethbridge from the Isles of Scilly right?' 'Yes Sir.' 'You have been posted overseas?' 'Yes Sir.' 'Do you want to go?' To which I replied that I did not mind, as I really did not want to spend the rest of the war at home. He then says that he didn't think I would go because my station had posted me, but the Air Ministry had lent me to the Royal Navy, and this posting should not have happened. There was quite a fuss about it but a signal was being sent through the channels to stop the posting.

About twenty-five years after this incident I was on the pier one day when a gentleman came over to me asking about the old ruins on Samson Island with the rocks close on the Southern side. He then told me that he was here once during the war when he was flying. 'It was thick fog at the time,' he said. I stopped him and asked, 'Were you in Sunderland flying boats?' He was quite surprised at the question and answered that he had been. I then told him that I would finish the story for him, which I did. He agreed with all that I told him but could not remember hearing me on the radio. He then realised that as he was the co-pilot he would not have heard it, only the pilot or wireless operator would have heard me talking.

A few years after that an Australian chap spoke to me one day when I was on the beach, asking about a hotel that was used for billeting aircrew at times during the war. I found out that our paths had also crossed before in Scilly, also that he knew the previous pilot well and had been to their reunion dinner with him the year before!

Anyway, when I arrived home after the court marshal my papers were there with the travelling warrants to report to the kitting out centre in Morcombe and so I caught the next morning's boat and was on my way. We did not know where we were going until we landed in Freetown West Africa. The ship we went out on was a new 69 thousand ton liner called the *Louis Pasteur*, she was very fast with her day speed being 29 knots but at dusk when we increased speed she would really start to vibrate. After the first 48 hours the destroyers escort left and we were on our own until 48 hours out of Freetown. We met some real bad weather at one spell and for 4 days nearly everyone was seasick.

Out of the 16 on our mess table there was only two of us for breakfast, so each morning we were faced with 32 boiled eggs between us. As I never had been seasick I was having a great time. The other chap was an R.A.F. Policeman called Charlie, on the last day of the bad weather we were out between the decks watching the sea. When it came to 3 o'clock N.A.F.F.I. time I said, 'Come on Charlie, let's get some tea'. He said he didn't fancy going below so I told him that I would bring him a mug of tea and a bun. When I returned he was gone, I searched and could not find him; this worried me because when I left him he was leaning on the rail being sick. I then reported it to the ship's orderly room and they said as it was now evening I was to keep looking as I was the only one that knew what he looked like. There was no point in a police search, but I was excused boat drill in the morning which all troops etc. attended every day at sea, but if he did not turn up for that he must be considered 'Lost at sea'. While boat drill was taking place, I found him lying on some ropes in a narrow dark area. I rushed him down to the orderly room where we found that as boat drill was now over they had just made out the signal ready to send that he had been 'Lost at sea'. Charlie and his wife came to see us many years after, and we had a laugh about it.

We were landed at Freetown and went to a transit camp up on the hill for about ten days, and then shipped on another ex-cattle ship, which was now turned into a coastal troop ship. The draft I was with were sent down to the bottom hold forward, there was hardly room to move when the hammocks were slung, and there were gratings over the hold – I suppose to allow the air in for us to breathe, as there certainly was not enough ventilation to support a few hundred men. There were only two single iron rung ladders to get out if we met any trouble. At that time there was quite a bit of submarine activity around the Freetown area, and so although it was against the rules, I decided no way was I spending the night in that trap, and so I used to find a corner on the main deck in the shelter and kip down.

We were on the way to Takoradi, the trip lasted about four or five days and again we managed to meet some very poor weather. The latrine for us consisted of two metal troughs leading to a pipe which ran out each side of the foredeck into the sea, but in the bad weather one could not get anywhere near the foredeck because of the sea breaking over the bow. There was a room on the main between-deck and as I needed to go somewhere I went to visit this room. When I got there the door was open and there was about six or eight toilets against one side wall and some wash basins around the others, but there were men sitting on the toilets so seasick that they didn't care about the water and vomit etc. that was washing around their legs up to about eighteen inches deep. As the ship rolled one way the sea came in over the doorsill, which was nearly knee high, then as she rolled the other way it went out again, needless to say I found another place to do the necessary.

The day after getting to Takoradi where there was an air base, also an Air Sea Rescue base I was sent on to Abidjan on the French West African Ivory Coast by an Anson aircraft delivering the stores for the detachment station of about 50 men. Abidjan consisted of a bunch of Nissen huts by the side of a lagoon, with a short wooden T-shaped pier where there was two or three seaplane tenders, a bomb scow (barge), one or two marine tenders, a refueller, and 3 or 4 mooring buoys for any flying boats that came in. This was an emergency landing base for flying boats that were short of fuel after their convoy patrol or submarine patrols, and of course if they were in any other trouble. The main trouble I found was the heat and the boredom. Sometimes we would go for weeks without seeing an aircraft except for a small French flying boat that used to come in about twice a week. She was much like a Catalina but a lot smaller, and after landing on the lagoon she would drop her wheels and run up their slipway, which was about half a mile down the lagoon from us. She normally did not affect us in any way but on one occasion was to give me one of the biggest scares I have ever had. We had been informed that a Sunderland was due to land that morning for fuel and it was my job to act as control boat in one of the seaplane tenders. All this usually consisted of was to make sure that the landing area was clear of native canoes, or any other logs or flotsam, and then wait for the aircraft to come in low over the trees at the end of the lagoon. On this particular day we had cleared the landing area and were ready to run along with her as she landed. As she came in over the trees I flashed her the normal green 'all clear to land' signal, but a few seconds later, the small French aircraft appeared coming in to land as well, a little behind and above the Sunderland. The first instinct was to flash a red, but I realised that if I did there would more than likely be a mid-air disaster. Because knowing the layout of both, I realised that the Sunderland pilot could not see the French aircraft because of the overhang of the cockpit roof, and also the French aircraft could not see the Sunderland below him because of it's boat shaped bow. I also realised that their landing speeds were similar, and therefore if I waited with everything firmly crossed, there was a chance that as the Sunderland touched the water the spray would be seen each side below the French aircraft's bow, and so very scared I decided to do nothing but to wait. Luckily that was what occurred. As the Sunderland touched down the French aircraft saw the spray and shot up in the air and so all was well. This was a situation where if there had been a collision I was sure to have been blamed one way or another, but luckily by doing nothing it must have saved many lives, although it frightened me nearly to death myself.

There was another time some of us had a bit of a scare. At one end of the main part of the L-shaped lagoon there was a narrow neck of land with the sea on the other side. On occasions we used to take a swimming party down to this strip of land, then cross over for a swim in the sea as it was forbidden to swim in the lagoon. To swim in the sea was risky because of Barracuda, sharks and angelfish, also there was always surf, which could build up very quickly at times to become very dangerous. This was exactly what happened while a bunch of us were swimming one afternoon.

As soon as the surf started to build up all the boys that were inshore got out of the water. One of our other coxswains, George Dimmock who was a very good swimmer, and myself were a bit further offshore, so we decided to wait a while for it to subside. The water was warm but after what must have been an hour or more we realised that we would have to risk coming in because the light would soon be going. We waved to those ashore that we were coming in and they formed chains as far out as they could into the surf to help us out. I have never felt anything like it before or since – I just did not know what was happening. I was rolled up in a ball, thrown around and did not know which way I was facing or if I was going up or down, until each time I was slammed down onto the hard sand, or when I broke surface with just time to grab a breath. George suffered the same treatment but we were both lucky to get in close enough for the other chaps to help us ashore.

As we were leaving two French army chaps arrived and we told them that the surf was too big. They did not take any notice of the warning because the following day we were told that they were both drowned.

George was a good mate, he was very easy going, nothing seemed to upset him much and he was always ready for a bit of fun. I remember I had a couple of chaps in my hut that used to put on the style a bit, although it was very obvious that they were a couple of 'fur coat and no drawers' cases and George decided that he could not stand it any longer. He had come down from his own hut to see me about something and had walked into a story these two were telling of a party they had had and something also about the posh tablecloths. George looked side on to me saying, 'My God, did you hear that Titch? We were lucky if we got a new newspaper as a tablecloth, weren't you?' I had a job to keep a straight face but managed to keep the sham going. These chaps swallowed it up hook, line and sinker, thinking they were in a different class to George altogether, when it was obvious that for all his fun and game it was the other way around. A few years ago I got in touch with him again and we are hoping to meet up sometime in the future – then 'the lamp will be swinging' as we used to say.

I had another lucky escape one morning while refuelling a Sunderland flying boat. The refuelers were forty-five feet long, steel boats – in fact they were just a big floating tank with a bow at one end and rudders and propellers at the other. There was a cockpit amidships with the engine and steering controls plus a pump engine, also all the pipes, valves and the meter to measure the fuel from the different tanks. We were literally surrounded by 100 % octane petrol.

On this particular day I had an inexperienced young deckhand with me on the after deck/tank, with a more experienced deckhand forward. If there was much wind or movement in the water we had to be careful going alongside, we would then lay under the plane's wing and pass the hoses up to the flight engineer who was responsible to see that the petrol did not overflow the filter cans. The excess would then drip off the trailing edge of the wing. I was in the cockpit when I heard this happening; I turned to look to see this new boy standing on the tank with a fag in his mouth, the matchbox in one hand and the match in the other. When I shouted he jumped nearly a foot high but at least he hadn't struck the match! When crewing on refuelers it was forbidden to carry any matches, lighters or metal objects – this was standing orders. He must have known and I suppose I should have checked, but I would lay a bet he never did it again after I had finished describing his parentage and upbringing. It still scares me when I think of it and I can still smell the fumes.

I also gave a few aircrew members plus our Squadron Leader C/O a bit of a fright around that time. I was towing in a Sunderland to the mooring buoys, the wind at the time was blowing quite fresh right across the lagoon, which made it very difficult. The big tail fin on these aircraft made them very hard to control when towing and particularly when turning down wind. I was faced with the problem of trying to do this with very little room to play with between the buoy and the sheer bank. Alternatively, I could try and tow her in between another Sunderland and the pier with only the same space as to the shore, but at that time I would still have control as long as I judged it right and as long as there was enough room. I decided that it was tight but possible, so I made for this gap.

When the aircrew saw what I was going to attempt to do, they got up on the wing and started shouting and waving their arms. The C/O plus his adjutant (whose office was just on the lagoon bank) came running down to the pier also waving and shouting, along with some of the boys coming to watch the fun. They were no doubt expecting to witness the cock-up of the century!

I was to say the least, a little concerned about the amount of room, but as long as there was room for the float on the wing to pass the pier, while the two wing tips of the Sunderlands passed each other it would be under control. After I got through I knew that I would only have to ease off the towing, then the Sunderland would automatically head up into the wind and it would be a piece of cake to moor it on the buoy.

As we passed between the other aircraft and the pier, one could have jumped from one wing tip to the other. At the same time the other wing was passing over the top of the pier while the wing float just slid past with very little room to spare. I then had her completely under control and moored her onto the buoy with no trouble at all.

When I looked around everyone had disappeared – some of the boys having missed a good laugh, the C/O having survived without having a heart attack, while I wore the grin of a Cheshire cat!

Abidjan was a very depressing place if you allowed it to be, but luckily we had a good bunch of blokes. We played football at times, but the most annoying thing was that down at Takoradi there were really good sports facilities and sports gear. After begging many times for them to send us up a couple of footballs as ours were splitting open, I gave up hope turned ours inside out and re-sewed it, and it lasted and was still there when we left. I remember making goal nets as well, but as a parent station they did not look after us very well. We were supposed to have two flights a week with mail and rations. I remember one time we were nearly six weeks without any. Lots of times we would be out of sugar, tea, fags, and beer and many other things. There was no milk of any sort, powder or tinned, real fresh milk we never had or expected, and only ever had real meat or real potatoes once in fourteen months – this was rolled brisket and it was for Christmas. When it was dished up cold, the rings of fat were full of fat juicy maggots, so we scraped out the rings of fat and ate the beef, and then had some fun trying to find who had the fastest and who had the biggest maggot.

Depression was treated as an illness and was taken very seriously by the Medical Officer and his orderly – the cook got it very badly. He was normal, one of the boys when he first arrived, but gradually got quiet and at times awkward. One day while some of us were sitting at the table he came to the serving counter, picked up a bucket of water and threw it all over our dinner and us. He became a liability and because we were only a small number there was no way he could be watched and looked after, also we needed a cook and so he was sent back to Takoradi. Whilst there he attempted to drown himself and also cut his own throat with a razor blade whilst in the toilet with his permanent police guard outside, but they caught him in time and eventually he was sent home on the trooper.

One time we were even out of fresh water and only had enough to drink for three or four days. We put up without washing our clothes or our bodies, which were always running in sweat and so we were really dirty and smelling awful. The lagoon was only about 20 to 50 yards away from any of the huts but this was full of bugs and things that got in one's ears and up the nose etc. being very dangerous to health, and in parts there were many crocodiles. Some of the boys would go off in the canoes with the natives shooting them for the skins, which the natives would dry and as a reward they would have the meat. We tried some roasted in the cookhouse one time, but it was not very nice. Because of all these things it was a station order that swimming etc. in the lagoon was a chargeable offence. After three or four days without a wash some of us decided that charge or no we were going in, there was about a dozen or more and so we thought that the C/O (whose office was just up the top of the pier on the lagoon bank) would not be able to put us all on a charge because the station would be in a non-operational state. So grabbing our towels and soap we went down the pier and jumped in and of course the C/O and his adjutant heard and saw us and came down telling us to get out immediately. We refused and explained that some of us had bad sores etc. – in fact I had some on both knees where I had fallen down and until I tied a three cornered handkerchief above them (to keep off the flies) there were live maggots on my knees. The C/O got fed-up threatening us and finally jumped in saying, 'Lend me your soap.' The other officer did likewise and everyone was satisfied. For all these sort of troubles we were a very close and in general a very happy bunch, like a very big family who could usually see the funny side whatever happened.

Eventually the war in Europe was over and in any case my 14 months were up so I was waiting for the boat home (this was only a 14 month station, at the time it was considered too unhealthy etc. for a longer period). We then closed the camp and everything was left for the French army or somebody.

Many of us with all our kit were put on a Dakota aircraft which was well overloaded. We revved up to full revs, took off the brake and tore up the landing strip, which was cut out of the trees. Before we got anywhere near the end of the runway, even <u>we</u> realised that she would never lift off and sure enough, with a screaming of brakes we stopped just short of the trees. Thinking then that they would unload some of us we were all much happier, but the pilot just went back, turned around and revving up again went tearing up the runway, lifting off but chopping off some of the branches on the way as we got airborne. During the flight we flew through a tropical storm when the wings were flapping like a seagull's, and the lightning was running all over them. On landing at Takoradi we zigzagged along with each wing tip in turn just clearing the ground while the fire engine and meat wagon (ambulance) tore along on each side of us waiting for the crash, which much to our relief did not happen. After leaving the aircraft we found that the tail wheel had spun the wrong way round, which was the cause of the hair raising return to the ground.

We were being brought home on a ship that years before was condemned for trooping but fit for native troops on the coast. At the time we came home she had been condemned for this and was being sent home for scrapping, so her iron decks were rusted right through and from underneath you could see the wood decks except for some edges of rusty iron. The cockroaches were everywhere and at night when in one's hammock just about a couple of feet overhead, the deck head was full of great monsters. We called in at Dakar and picked up some more servicemen and had some engine repairs, we also went in both to Casablanca, which was a really filthy harbour for repairs and again at Gibraltar for more engine repairs. The trip home lasting three weeks against 10 days going out, and the food on the way home was really bad but nevertheless we were on our way home so to hell with it.

We arrived in Southampton on a Saturday, early evening and it was strange to see all the lights and hear the music coming from off the land, but we were not allowed ashore until Sunday morning when we were sent to West Kirby to be re-kitted out and sent on leave. While on leave I received my posting orders to find that I was to stay in Scilly in charge of the tender again but now with a base on Rat Island and four or five other chaps as my staff. The reason that I had been posted straight back to Scilly was because there had been quite a fuss between the Air Ministry and the Royal Navy as I had been lent to them until they decided that I was no longer needed and the skipper of the High Speed Launch had been immediately posted to the Shetland Isles at the time as a punishment for causing all the trouble. The Royal Navy had also been promised that as soon as I returned from West Africa I was to be returned to them.

There was very little to do as all the other boats had left and there were no Sunderlands calling in or anything happening, but we did have one trip, which was a bit out of the ordinary. One morning between ten and eleven o'clock we had a phone call from Air Ministry itself, whoever it was said that there was a four engine aircraft, I believe a Halifax, missing in the area. It's track was to pass 15 miles North West of the Bishop Lighthouse on it's nearest point, there was an aircraft searching for it and would I be willing to go and rescue any survivors or anything if the aircraft spotted it as they said they knew we only had a small boat on the station. I told him that we certainly would and so we took some extra diesel oil in five-gallon tins aboard and waited. It was about four o'clock in the afternoon before we heard from them saying that the search aircraft had sighted what they considered was wreckage 42 miles North West of the Bishop Lighthouse and so from St. Mary's this made it about 48 miles – were we still willing to go? I agreed that we were and so off we went in this 24 foot marine tender which now had a small canvas wheelhouse but was an open boat with a speed of about 14 knots and only a compass and watch to help us. There was a wireless officer on call on St. Mary's and two telescopic aerial masts, but after getting away from the Islands a bit we lost contact, this was on return found out to be because they had forgotten to wind up the masts to their full extent. We found the aircraft with no trouble and he was flying around the wreckage. When we got there we found it was only a lot of floating seaweed with bits of wood and general flotsam and so after informing the aircraft he said that he was returning to his base and we were to return to ours. The wind was now freshening from the South East dead ahead and we were throwing a lot of spray aboard. The boat was banging about quite a bit and then the engine stopped out of fuel. As it was now dark and we had all been up under the shelter we had not noticed how much water we were taking onboard. When we stopped, the water ran forward and we realised that we had taken on a lot of water, after pumping out and refuelling we again set off for the Bishop. We did not sight the light as expected but I realised that the weather etc. was slowing us down a lot and all of a sudden there was a flashing light right ahead. Within a very short time we were up to what turned out to be a fishing boat's marker buoy with a lantern on it, which had been going up and down behind the waves. This did not help as we should have now been into the Bishop and some of the boys were getting really worried and seasick. They were wrapped up in some blankets we had taken with us for anyone we found and they were now talking of what may happen to us if we could not make the Bishop Lighthouse. This was annoying me and so when I did sight it I did not tell them but waited until we were right under it and then said, 'Now you can stop your moaning because there's the Bishop up there above us.' I then turned to Port and headed for where the Old Wreck buoy was, the time about 2 o' clock in the morning when we should have reached the Bishop at about half past twelve if the wind had not altered and freshened up. It was also drizzling, with poor visibility and I was hoping that we would hit the buoy O.K., as it had no light. The next thing I saw was a big black shape and so I shut off the throttle and turned hard to port, we had nearly actually ran into the buoy. As I opened up again the engine started surging badly and so I knew the air had got into the fuel line because of the tanks being nearly empty and the change of trim of the boat when we eased down quickly. So for approximately the next three miles I was praying that we would make the harbour. Although we would have been all right, it would have been a great disappointment to have to be towed in after a trip of about a hundred miles, plus having the weather turning against us and so we surged our way home to the harbour steps. Before the chaps had stepped ashore the engine stopped, I dipped the tank and it was really empty. When I got home that night, I peeped in Dad's bedroom to let him know that we were back all right, thinking he may be at least a bit worried. On finding that he was fast asleep I had to grin to myself and thought it was quite a compliment to know that he had that amount of confidence in my being able to cope. The morning after our long trip we received a telegram of congratulations and thanks on the effort we had put in, although to no avail. The wireless officer went to London on leave shortly afterwards and on his return he said to me, ' You caused some trouble over that trip, you did.' He had visited Air Ministry in London while on leave and he was told that I was to have been mentioned in dispatches. However, when it was sent through the channels the Air Sea Rescue inspector whom I had had trouble with at Newlyn, hit the roof and wanted me court marshalled for breaking the Air Ministry's own standing orders that this type of boat was not allowed to go any further than 3 miles from base wherever it may be. So, as they had congratulated us on breaking their own rules they could now neither award or punish me for it and so decided to push it under the table and forget it had ever happened. This still makes me grin, thinking of the inspector that I had got the better of on both of the occasions that I had been involved with him, plus most likely the posting overseas problem. He must have loved to hear my name mentioned.

One morning one of the boys told me that the land girls on Tresco were having a dance on the island and that they were invited to attend if they could find a way to get there. They wanted to know if I would take them up in the boat and then pick them up after the dance. It was, of course, against all the rules and I knew that if there were any trouble or damage done I would have no excuse at all. I told them that I would do it as long as they promised to take a torch with them to guide me in at Carn Near (there was no proper pier there at that time). I also said that they must be there at 12.30 am and no later.

Everything was agreed and they invited the Flight Lieutenant wireless officer who was attached to us to go with them. I took them all up and then returned at about 12.15 am and waited. There was no sign of them at 12.30 am but I managed to get into the landing place in the dark without even any moonlight. I then waited for about half an hour when I could hear singing and laughter – results of the Tresco coffee of course. This was soon followed by lots of shouting and waving of lights. I managed to get them all aboard and returned to St. Mary's pier where the boys remembered how things should be done. They invited the officer who, to say the least in the morning would never remember anything, to get ashore first. He forgot to wait until the boat was properly alongside; he then stepped very elegantly into the water between the boat and the pier. He crawled out onto the steps, put his cap back on, thanked me very much for the lovely evening he had enjoyed and continued to crawl up the steps on his hands and knees, accompanied by roars of laughter.

After closing down in Scilly I was again sent on a 1st class coxswain's course to Coreswal camp which, not having crossed paths with the Squadron Leader who I had upset before, I passed with good marks. History repeated itself in that as I had been told when I passed my 2nd class course that I was the youngest coxswain in the Air Force, I was told again that I was probably the youngest 1st coxswain and was now posted to Invergorden in Scotland. Once again I would go from living at home, to just about as far away in Britain as I could be. I was for a short period sent to Loch Goilhead where the Navy submarine branch was and is now I think called Faselaine. The reason being that I was to relieve a Sergeant 1st Cox, in charge of a small base of about five or six men, a fast 18 foot motor dinghy, a rowing dinghy, an iron barge with corrugated iron shed covering it inboard, and a sixty foot general purpose Pinnace.

We lived in an old farmhouse on the banks of the Loch and catered for ourselves. Our job was to tend on some civilian boffins who were working on a new aircraft torpedo that when dropped would follow the propeller noises of a ship and destroy the ship. It was a hush-hush job. We were quite happy to get along together well, we more or less shared what cleaning and cooking etc. that was necessary and if one of the chaps was very good at cooking or anything then he would do most of that particular chore. One time when we were out of bread there was talk of trying to bake some for ourselves and as none of them had any idea of how to do it they turned to me, 'Do you know anything about bread making Titch?' Although I was now a sergeant, I was still known as Titch unless there were any officers etc. around. I had to admit that I did, as my mother always made our own bread and so asked for the flour, milk, salt and yeast. 'Oh we haven't got any yeast,' the boys say, but someone reckoned we could use baking powder in place of yeast. So I made some bread rolls and everyone couldn't wait to have a laugh at my baking, but although it was not of catering standards they were quite surprised, and it kept us going until we could get our rations.

Twice a week I would take the Pinnace with two or three of the boys around to Helensborough for rations, this made a bit of an outing for us. On one of the trips we were approaching the main part of the Clyde and we could see some tugs towing something but could not decide what it was. As it got closer it turned out to be the first war German battle-ship *Derflinger* upside down with a big tin shed built on it – I suppose for the towing crew to live in while on the passage. It was really queer with the shed, and rudder and props all on top of what looked like a submarine from a distance.

After about a couple of months I returned to Alness, which was the station at Invergorden. We did a variety of jobs, again clearing up after the war, dumping all sorts of now not required stores out in the Loch using a bomb scow. I also remember taking one of three 'refuelers' to Inverness.

One night when I was duty coxswain I was in the pier office trying to keep awake, as in this small hut there was just a desk with telephone and necessary books and an old coke-burning stove. As it was cold and windy I had shut the door, the window was non-opening, and the coke in the stove had been sprayed with diesel oil as usual and so I was snug and warm. I dozed off, but luckily something outside woke me. On waking I was very mixed up and the room was stifling hot and smoky with diesel fumes but I managed to get to the door and out into the fresh night air – I was a very lucky bloke.

Another night when we were duty crew, as it was about nine o'clock, I told the boys that we would leave the youngest one to make the supper while we went around the boats checking that all was well for the night. Before we had left the pier to check the boats on the moorings he came to tell us that the supper was ready. I thought, 'That was quick,' but said, 'OK, we might as well have it now.' We returned to the crew hut where I was to find that he had put our entire tea ration in the pot and had then filled the pot with COLD water from the tap! He was not the most popular bloke around. I just could not believe anyone could be so stupid as to not know how to make tea. Maybe he came from a rich family with bags of servants – if so he was in for a terrible time until he was educated into service life.

One morning the Commanding Officer called me up to his office, 'Have you ever done any target towing?' he asks. 'Yes Sir, quite a lot when I was on the East Coast,' I reply. 'Well Kinlass air station have phoned requesting a target towing boat to be on the range for a bombing exercise programme by nine o'clock tomorrow morning. Can you manage it as none of the other coxswains have done any target towing?' 'That's no problem Sir.' He then says that an officer will be arriving to go with us as a control and safety officer in the morning, to which I replied that this Officer must be there by 6.45 am, to give us time to get down to the range (off Torbart Ness Light) and get rigged for towing, ' I will inform them now,' he says, ' And thank-you.'

The next morning we were all ready and alongside the pier waiting for the safety officer by 6.45 am as arranged. Seven o'clock came, 7.15 am and 7.30 am and by this time I knew we would have to cut corners to make it by 9 o'clock, and so I told the crew to cast off saying, 'We never ever had any bloody safety officer before so we will go without him,' and off we went. We arrived and were just ready to go when the first aircraft arrived. We spent the day towing for several different Lancasters and about five o'clock the last aircraft called us up thanking us for a very good and successful programme wishing us goodnight and 'you may return to base'. As we were getting close to the pier we could see someone walking up and down the end of the pier, as the day boys were already off duty I said to the boys, 'Look out for it now, I'll bet that's the damned safety officer.' As soon as we get alongside he started shouting at me and saying what he was going to do to me for going without him, again I would be court marshalled and so on, again this was my third time and so I waited until he ran out of steam and then went to town. He was a Flight Lieutenant and I was only a Sergeant but I reminded him that he had not been there by

My Pinnace crew, myself 3rd from right.

7.30 am at least and as we had done the job without him if he had one atom of sense in his head, he would return to Kinlass as if nothing had happened. I told him about the signal we had received and I said that everyone was happy and no one knew that he had not been present. I said, 'If you have any sense at all you will say nothing because if I am in trouble you will be in the shit up to your armpits, I will make sure of that, now bugger off and do what you like.' He did just that and I heard no more about it.

Eventually my demob number came up again. I had already had my demob postponed for two three month stretches and up to now I had always managed to avoid going on an N.C.O.'s course (which was really a drill, stores, and office management etc. course) by some means or other, but could see I would get caught very soon. At this time there were more peacetime parades etc. creeping in and as I had no time for that sort of thing I was looking forward to going home. When I only had two weeks to go the C/O once again sent for me. 'I have a favour I would like you to do for me,' he said, and I of course was expecting some special job concerning the boats but he then said, 'I believe you are due for demob in two weeks time.' 'That's right Sir.' 'Well I have a favour to ask you. I am due for demob myself in three months time and if you would sign on for another three months you can put this on your arm right now.' As he said it he pushed a Flight Sergeant Crown on the desk, 'As I would like you to stay while I am here.' I don't hardly know how I felt – firstly very surprised, also very pleased to think that he should say that he appreciated how I did my job and then really sorry to have to tell him that even the promotion could not keep me in now that the war was over. I just said that I was very, very sorry but I was in a hurry to get home and get the boat and myself ready for the coming fishing season. He was disappointed but nevertheless wished me well and when I left he gave me my final pay book report and reference, when he wrote: The above named N.C.O. is a keen and conscientious worker, a good N.C.O. and always on top of his job. R.A.F. character V.G., which is of the highest that can be awarded in the R.A.F. I was quite pleased and proud of this especially when I think of the many times I broke the rules and simply got away with it, because I proved myself right.

Before I leave this part of my story, I must say that in general I would not have missed my service time for anything. I served under some very good officers and a few poor ones. I met and served with a great bunch of chaps many of which I still often think of, and some of whom I have been lucky enough to meet again throughout the years. During my time as both an Airman and an N.C.O. I was never on a charge and never put anyone else on a charge. I always did my share of anchor watches and other chores and on the only occasion that I was let down (some of the chaps thought I was going to hit this particular chap), one of them grabbed me and said, 'No, no Titch that's what he would love you to do, leave him to us and we will sort him out, don't worry.' – and I suppose they did, Bless Them All.

I arrived home a free man again just before Christmas 1946 and I remember quite well saying to a mate as I left the demob centre, 'Well that's the last time I say Sir to anyone unless I want to,' and so it has been, without I hope being offensive but with a feeling of as a man, (Jack is as good as his master).

CHAPTER 5

AFTER THE WAR

D AD HAD written to me saying that he could now have the *J.M.L.* back from the Government at a good price and as he did not want her, he wanted to know if I were interested, which he knew I was so he would get her back for me. I was on leave when he was allowed to pick her up and so I met him in Penzance and returned home with her. Also on leave at the time were two of my school mates, one Air Force A.S.R., Roy Jenkins and one Army, Frankie Hicks, who were stranded in Penzance because they had both missed the *Scillonian* the local steamer to the Islands and so they hitched a lift with us. We had had quite a dirty trip and although cold, wet, and hungry we were all glad to be home.

When the blokes returned from the different services, sport became a big thing. There had always been a cricket club but now football took off in a big way. We eventually had four teams, two from St. Mary's (the Rovers and the Rangers), also one each from Tresco and St. Martins. This allowed us to play one home and one away match each Sunday afternoon against a different team each week. We had a knock out cup and a league cup. The cup game would be held on the St. Mary's ground when there would be all the supporters coming from the off islands plus the regulars. The edge of the field would be full and in some places two or three deep, some supporters had their coloured rosettes and rattles – it was good fun. When this was well established some non-players decided that we needed a committee to run things – soon after this, as usual all the arguments started, the sportsmanship disappeared, so did the players and the whole thing folded up. The same thing happened to our sailing club. This started with a few boats with Ginger Green as timekeeper and Joe Pender with his twelve bore shotgun to start and finish the races. It grew into two classes, 14 feet and 18 feet (approximately – no one worried much as long as it floated), and there weren't any special rules except the normal rules at sea. This club folded the same way as the football with some of the same non-players on the committee!

During the winter months I worked on the quay unloading the *Scillonian's* cargo and I remember helping unload the last coal boat. These were coasters usually around 300 tons cargo with a fixed agreed price to unload the cargo of coal by using their own derricks for one pound for each 100 ton. This was usually three days work but on this occasion there was something special happening on the afternoon of the third day and so we all agreed to get cracking and we finished her in two and a half days. The coal merchant then did not want to pay us more than two pounds ten shillings, but he soon found out different.

Uncle Jim had now finished under the Navy and had been working a few pots on his own in his boat the *Kestrel* and Dad had a yarn with him and persuaded him that it would be to all our advantage to go together in the *J.M.L.* It was all hard work at that time and pulling pots in 30–40 fathoms of water sometimes, was real hard going. Our hands would be red raw at times and when dry would split at the joints. When we went three handed, we could work the deeper better grounds and all benefit, our Uncle because we could do the main hauling while he did most of the cleaning and baiting, and as he would be the boss or skipper we would get the benefit of his knowledge, which money could not buy.

My Dad was still the coxswain of the lifeboat and Uncle Jim had been, and still was 2nd coxswain since before I was born. Harry and I had both joined the crew as some of the older men, who had come back to serve on the boat during wartime, were ready to finish. My brother Richard had also joined the crew and so there was now, Dad coxswain, Uncle Jim 2nd coxswain, Tom Bodilly as bowman, and myself and two brothers as crewmembers. Henry Thomas as chief engineer was the only full time paid man; the 2nd mechanic was Waldron Phillips (also returned from Navy services). Within a short time Tom, because of illness, had to finish and so I was made bowman. Of course over the years there would be many changes to come. My first real trip in the lifeboat had been to Plymouth, taking the boat for refit when I was 14 years old, and I believe some of the men were surprised to find that I was not seasick. It was no surprise to either Dad or Uncle Jim, as I often went fishing with them.

I was the only one allowed to go fishing because I didn't get seasick, and although only a boy my help on the hauling was very welcome. So I pulled my heart out to make sure I could go again the next day. This of course was only during school holidays or Saturdays, and not if it was really dirty weather. The fishing after the war was mainly for crayfish or lobsters, crabs were of no value at all. Lobsters were worth about one shilling a pound and crayfish, one shilling and three pence a pound. On very good days we could catch over 100 crayfish and maybe about 30–40 lobsters, out of 75 pots. We packed our fish in barrels and sent them over by the *Scillonian* to a merchant in Newlyn. We got our returns in cash (there was no Income Tax in the Islands at that time) every Saturday, in a brown envelope by courtesy of the Bosun of the steamer. We then had a share up in our store, which was just a three way split after expenses, any odds were saved by me, in what we called the 'boat's box' for immediate expenses.

The time I spent with my uncle stood me in good stead in the years to come. We got on very well together and when it was risky to haul a string of pots because of the weather and the closeness of a ledge of rocks, I being a bit young and probably foolish, would try to egg him on to have a go at it. Afterwards he would say, 'One of these days boy you will drown yourself.' I expect at these times he was thinking of his two brothers Alfred and George, 21 and 29 years old who were both drowned while out fishing.

My uncle and brother Harry and I fished for five years, and I believe except for one occasion, never had a cross word, in fact in all the time I spent with Uncle Jim. I know as far as he was concerned I couldn't do a thing wrong except for this one time. We were measuring out the ropes ready to tar them, each string of pots needed three lengths of rope to be joined later, to make up a length of 15 pots. I said, 'O.K. that will be two 46 fathoms and one 50 fathoms.' He disagreed but I knew that if we cut the ropes to the lengths he wanted, we would make a real mess of it. After trying to explain many times why it must be as I said, he turned to Harry and said, 'Come on boy, we don't know anything so leave him to it,' and so I had to make up all the ropes ready for tarring. The next day we did the tarring by dipping each coil in boiling tar and nothing was said about the measures, neither when we joined them together, when everything worked out right, or at anytime afterwards. I reckon he had realised when he got home that I was right, but no way was he going to say so after the fuss we had had. Probably it was a good thing in the long run, because we never had another harsh word.

One morning on the 10th June 1949, around nine o'clock we were hauling our pots at Bishop Ridge when we heard the lifeboat rockets, as we were so far away and as there were no such things as V.H.F. radios, echo sounders, or radar etc. we had to wait to find out what it was all about until we got home. As it had been a bit foggy we did wonder if a ship had gone ashore, and on getting home we found out that a ship had gone on the Seven Stones rocks about seven miles North East of St. Martins Island. It was a fine day other than the early bit of fog. The lifeboat and one of the Steamship Company boats had returned, the ship's crew had abandoned the ship in their own lifeboat, which the Steamship boat (being faster than the lifeboat) had met and taken on board. We found out that the ship was a cargo ship of 6,369 tons called the *Fantee*, and was loaded with logs from West Africa, which were of Mahogany, Teak and other hard woods. The lifeboat engineer said that she was still above water but cracking in half and so we grabbed something to eat and took on an extra five-gallon can of fuel, some extra rope and big 4 and 6-inch nails. Off we go in the *J.M.L.* to try and salvage some logs, which we (Uncle Jim, Henry Thomas, Harry and myself) and everyone else thought, would be worth quite a lot of money.

On arrival we found logs floating everywhere, and so made the first one fast towing it, until we found another nice big one and we carried out the same task. As we made fast to each log we were having more of a struggle to tow, we were also now plastered in thick fuel oil from the ship's tanks that had burst open. After getting four logs in tow we decided to make for home, at a very slow speed. At the time there were also a lot of bales of raw cotton drifting around, which the boats were ignoring, as we thought these would not be worth much. On the way home, about half way I should think, a passenger launch passed us towing two small logs. She was a much bigger and a more powerful boat than ours, but soon after passing us, one of their smaller logs parted the rope, but they just left it and carried on with the one log. We of course could not leave this and also made fast to it, and again started for home at a crawling pace. We now decided to tip our spare fuel into the tanks but as I picked up the can I found it was just about empty. What had happened was, while struggling to make fast to the logs someone had knocked over the can, the top had come off and as everything was smothered and stinking of oil, none of us had noticed. Now we were in trouble, the wind was also freshening and we knew that the tide would also turn against us later. Soon after we parted one log and decided to leave it, as we knew we were going to have a job to get home before running out of fuel. We eventually ended up with one log, still not knowing if we would make St. Martins before the tide changed. There was another boat the *Verona* with Mr. Bert Jenkins and his son on board coming behind us with two logs. We just got in out of the tide (which had now turned) before it became too strong and we could see that the *Verona* was being carried away to the North and would now have to go right up around St. Martins. We still had our own troubles wondering if we were going to make it, but we just managed to get in after dark and with just about empty tanks.

The next morning we found out from the Customs Officer that the cotton was worth quite a lot of money, and the logs worth very little. Undeterred off we go again after the cotton bales, which yesterday were plentiful and floating very light in the water. Now they were hard to find, and floating deep and very heavy. We could not get them aboard, and so lashed them along the sides and got eight of them home like that. Bert and Roy were also doing the same thing. The ship had broken in half on the first night and had gone to the bottom, and so our total reward was one log and eight bales of cotton, which were now not worth very much. So, except for having the memories and laughs about it, we had very little else.

Uncle Jim, Myself and Harry.

CHAPTER 6

MARRIED LIFE AND THE LIFEBOAT

OR THE last three years or so I had been going out with Pat, a local girl that I knew when we were both at school. As she still keeps reminding me, she was two and a half years younger than me, and therefore I did not really know her until I came home at the end of the war. We both loved dancing, and at that time there was always one dance in the Town Hall every Saturday night, at 8.00 pm. It always finished at 11.45 pm to get everything closed up before Sunday morning. The entrance fee was one shilling, and then quite often there was a sixpenny hop (as it was called) in the Church Hall on Wednesdays. I had been watching Pat dancing, and could see that she was good; also that she was always laughing and enjoying herself. So I took the biggest step I have ever taken in my life, and one, which I was, and always will be thankful for, by asking her to dance, from then on we never looked back.

Pat lived up at the other end of the Island and at first she would come in on the bus, and return on the same. Shortly after I bought an ex-Army motorbike, it was a 350cc Royal Enfield. At first she was not very keen, but eventually got quite used to it, and except for hanging on like grim death and the endless record of, 'Slow down a bit, you're going too fast,' the motorbike was a great help. Many times if I had stayed up at Telegraph after about 11 o'clock, I would switch it off at Carn Thomas and freewheel as far as I could, then push it the rest of the way, otherwise I would have been told off for waking up the town.

One other thing I shall never forget, and although it shows how stupid I was, I have spoken of this and had many laughs about it over the years. One evening when I was going up the road towards Pat's house the engine spluttered once or twice and then stopped. I thought that it couldn't be out of petrol, but on shaking the bike with the cap off the tank, I couldn't hear any sloshing about. It was dark and I couldn't see in the tank but thought I must not strike a match to see. However, as I could not find out any other way, I decided that if I held it well away from the opening, it might be O.K. As the match got closer for me to be able to see, there was a big whoosh, and a flash of blue flame, and the tank was on fire. I could now imagine the bike being blown to pieces, but knowing that fire can not survive without air, I caught hold of the handlebar with my left hand, standing as far away as I could, and put my right hand lightly over the flame coming out of the tank. I waited a while afraid to take my hand away, but wanting to run like the devil. When I took my hand away, I was more than happy to find the fire out, and I still had the bike!

Pat's father was then the Green Keeper for the Golf Links, and also grew flowers for the mainland. Her mother used to do the tying etc.; her brother Henry was learning his trade with the engineer of the lifeboat, Henry Thomas. As I was always going in and out of the engineer's shop, and sometimes working there at odd times, I soon knew all the Taylor family and became 'on the staff' as it were.

How Pat ever put up with me I don't know. Many times when we were supposed to be going somewhere, I would have to do something on the boat's engine etc. so that we were able to go to sea the next morning. Only those who have been involved with commercial fishing will ever understand how one's life is ruled by the weather and the tides. She never really complained, she was very disappointed sometimes but accepted it as it was. This made me more sure that she was the one for me. As I was not much of a sweet talker, one evening walking back to her place (I believe we were talking of my brother Harry, who was getting married to her friend Pam) I plucked up enough courage to say, 'Well I suppose we ought to get engaged.' By this time I suppose she knew me well enough to accept this sort of thing.

We were married on December 27th 1949 at 8 o'clock in the morning in the Methodist Chapel, the reason being that we were catching the small twin wing Rapide passenger plane to St. Just airport, and then going on to Birmingham to spend a couple of weeks with friends, and another week with my brother George and family in London. Neither of us were in any way very well off, but we had been collecting bits and pieces to make a home.

Thanks again to Pat, we had found two rooms, with the use of the kitchen, with an old lady who was very good to us for just over a year, when we were allocated one of the first lots of Council houses to rent. Our new home had two bedrooms, living room, and kitchen, with a small bathroom and of course separate toilet. We now had for the first time hot and cold water, as we wanted it. The water was heated by a Rayburn stove in the living room, which also was for cooking and heating, it was a real luxury. It meant that if I came home from the boat wet and cold, I could strip off and warm up with a nice hot bath.

Our first daughter Jean was born on the 16th January 1951, and on Pat's return from hospital with Jean we moved into our new home. Jean was a real big baby of 10lbs 2oz and we were now on top of the world.

In the winter months when it was no good for fishing, I always had plenty of work offered to me from all sorts of tradesmen, shipwrights, carpenters, builders, decorators and even the local blacksmith. All these jobs were a great help during my later life. I also worked as a stevedore on the *Scillonian*, or as skipper or crew with Dad on the cargo and passenger launch to the off islands.

Our wedding day left to right: Henry and Alice Taylor, Evelyn Thomas, Pat, Myself, Elaine Thomas, Richard, Aunty, Dad.

I have never had to ask for a job, and many times have been asked to stay or come back after the fishing season, neither have I ever been sacked.

The fishing had now dropped off, and my uncle decided that there was not enough in it for three men. As we now had a capstan for hauling, he decided that it would be easier for him if he got a shore job. He also had to finish as 2nd coxswain of the lifeboat, and I then took over from him as 2nd coxswain to Dad in the 'Cunard'. Harry decided to carry on fishing for another season with me, to see if it would improve.

That Christmas the B.B.C. had arranged to broadcast a Christmas message from the Bishop Rock Lighthouse, the last lighthouse in England. The broadcaster, Edward Ward and his engineer Charlie Coombs were taken down and put aboard on Christmas Eve, by the contractor for the lighthouses – Mr. Bert Jenkins and his son Roy in the *Verona*. The broadcast was a success, but the weather had turned nasty, making the relief not possible. They then became stuck on the Bishop. After about three weeks of bad weather, they were now all eating the keepers' iron rations. We were going on our normal six weekly exercise in the lifeboat, so it was arranged that we would take extra food to them but we were not intending to take off the B.B.C. men. Dad out of courtesy asked Bert and Roy if they would like to come with us, which they both agreed to do. We sent the food ashore by a rope from the winch on the

Galley at the top of the lighthouse, and before we knew what was happening Edward Ward was being lowered down on the rope! We got him aboard safely, and then the engineer followed. Afterwards we found out that they were supposed to have said that they had had enough of the Bishop and the bad weather, and the broadcaster had told the keepers that if they did not send him down on the rope, he would jump into the sea and the lifeboat would then have to pick him up.

On the way home Dad asked me if I would like Roy to stay aboard as a crew member in the lifeboat, seeing that Uncle Jim was finishing, and he himself would also be finishing before very long. Roy was pleased to come with us, and so I became 2nd coxswain, and Roy took my place as bowman. We did one or two jobs in fine weather, one of which was towing in a little steam puffer (coaster) from a couple of miles off Round Island, which had become disabled. Another service was to stand by a modern steam vessel *The Duke of Sparta*, a lovely ship of 7,176 tons, which was aground on one of the Seven Stones rocks. We took her first officer aboard the lifeboat, and with a lead line showed him the depth of water around the ship and the way out, if she floated off at high water. We then put my uncle aboard as a Pilot to advise when she was re-floated. When she was clear of the rocks we returned his lifeboats (which we had been towing), and picked up my uncle. With a tug which had arrived and which was engaged as an escort, he set off for Falmouth. The Board of Trade surveyor that surveyed her after the grounding later told us that there was a hole in her bottom plates big enough to take a double-decker bus through, and if her bulk head had not held, she would have gone to the bottom.

My first big test in charge of the lifeboat was in 1951, when the *Scillonian* went ashore in the thickest fog I have ever seen. She was on passage from Penzance to Scilly, the launch *Kittern* had gone out to meet her off Peninnis Head with my father as skipper. This was normal procedure in a thick fog and the launch would then help lead the steamer into harbour. There was no radar or position finding equipment available at that time, other than the log, compass, clock and revolution counter. The *Scillonian* however made a perfect landfall at Deep Point, and not realising how thick the fog was, the Captain decided to try getting into St. Mary's harbour.

Vic Trenwith was on Peninnis Head, blowing his bugle, which was again the normal practice, but the *Scillonian* did not hear it. Although the launch was hearing her fog signal, she could not catch her, but kept on chasing her past Porthcressa and on past St. Agnes. The Captain then realised that he had passed the entrance to St. Mary's Sound, so he turned back to the eastwards, a few minutes later with a crunch she ran onto the rocks.

I was at the time on the pier when the first lifeboat maroon exploded, those of us that were connected with the lifeboat jumped on a lorry and went to the boathouse. Henry Thomas the mechanic had been following the *Scillonian's* progress by keeping in touch with her wireless operator, who had reported her as being ashore on the Wingletang Ledges, at the South West corner of St. Agnes. I was now in charge for the first real service, with Roy Jenkins also for his first time as 2nd coxswain. We made good courses between the Island and rocks to the corner of St. Agnes, where we met the *Kittern* just on her way back. When they saw us they stopped and beckoned us towards them, Dad said that the *Scillonian* was hard ashore but all right, he was very overloaded with passengers from the *Scillonian* and asked us to take half of them aboard. We then both set off for St. Mary's. On the way back I could see he was always heading a bit farther East than myself, but knowing that when he picked up the shore he would alter course, I just kept my eye on her. When they sighted Rat Island at the back part of the harbour, I saw her stop, so I also stopped to see if he was O.K. He was clear of the rocks ahead, but on going astern to turn, the rudder was knocked off by hitting a single rock. We then took him in tow to the harbour – poor Dad had his leg pulled quite a lot over that.

Landing passengers from Scillonian.

1952 was a very bad year for us, the Doctor told Pat that she had Tuberculosis, and needed to go into hospital. Jean was only 18 months old, and a real bonny little girl, so this news was like the end of the world to us. Pat's first worries were if Jean or myself were also infected. After having some tests both Jean and I were found to be clear. Pat then went to Tehidy hospital and was to stay there for the next ten months. It was the worst time of our lives. Every now and then when she got very down, I would go over to the mainland for the weekend and tell her all the news about Jean. Pat's greatest fear was that Jean would forget her, but when she returned everything was all right. Of course now followed a long spell of convalescence and worrying, but luckily she recovered well and had not had to have any operations. I could never put into words what a relief it was when she was finally told that it was not necessary for her to have any more check ups.

Harry had finished fishing and so I was now faced with giving up, or going on my own. During this winter Mr. Bert Jenkins often came in my store and talked of getting a big passenger launch, and also giving up the fishing, but he was always saying that it needed to be three. I knew that he was suggesting that I join them, so that two of us could work in the big boat and the other one could be on his own in the smaller boat. Or we could take turns in the smaller one doing the special trips, and work all three together doing the Lighthouse contract.

On the Easter Monday of that year on going to quay, my Dad and cousin Jim (who was now working with him as engineer) found Bert floating face down in the water, and on picking him out found that it was already too late. It was found that he had had a brain haemorrhage or something and had fallen in and drowned.

Roy then went fishing with his uncle, and I did the unheard of thing in those days of going on my own. We did not have much money and so I bought six dozen pots and rigged out eight strings of eight pots in each string. By having only eight in a string, I was able to get into many more of the little corners between the rocks than we could with the longer strings. This made quite a difference to the fishing. As I was on my own I was working all the hours that God gave, including taking people out sailing in the afternoon in the *Kathleen*. She was a 32 foot yawl, built for my Granddad, passed on to my Dad, and after being refitted (as she was in a poor state at the end of the war) Dad gave her to me.

In the August of that year, in fact the 18th, on rowing out to the *J.M.L.* to go fishing, I happened to meet up with Roy and his uncle, also on the way to their boat. Roy was pulling and John was sat in the stern holding his oilskin on his lap. Jokingly I remarked that he would need his oilskin this morning, as there was just a fresh wind with very little ground sea. We set off for the Bishop and

Kathleen.

Crim areas together, them a little ahead of me. As I was going I was letting the boat steer herself and just checking by glancing around every now and then, while I cut up my pot bait. As I got down towards the Smiths rock, the boat fell into a trough a bit heavy so I looked at the white water around the rock, and thought to myself that there was a bit of Ground Sea after all. Shortly afterwards the boat again fell quite heavily, and on looking again I decided that there was quite a lot of sea after all. Within about fifteen to twenty minutes the sea had completely changed from a fresh breeze and a light sea, into a very fresh breeze but a real heavy sea. As I got to passing the Haycocks rocks on the end of Annet Island, the sea was now running right up over them and burying them under, right up to the grass on Annet. I had one string of pots just outside of Annet Head, close to an underwater ledge called George Peters Ledge. I was sure that if I did not rescue it there would be nothing of it left, but before I got there I could see that the whole area was a'boil with breaking water, right into the shore. At about this time I looked up to the North of me and saw Roy's boat with her mizzen sail and she seemed to be stopped, as if she was hauling. By this time I felt that I must save what gear I could and I then went down to the Gilstone, which is the most South Western rock where Sir Cloudesley Shovell was wrecked in 1707. When I got there everything now was breaking very heavily, so I knew that the main thing was to try and get back to the harbour. It was now the heaviest sea that I have ever seen either before or since. When I tried to get home on my usual routes, none of them were possible, and so I returned by going around the South of St. Agnes in the deep water and more sheltered from the Western and North Western sea, I then came up St. Mary's Sound and in towards the harbour. I was very worried to see if Roy and John were back in the harbour feeling that if they were not, there was not much chance of the boat returning. When I saw that their punt was still on the mooring but no sign of the boat, I was very afraid for them. On getting ashore I went to see Dad and told him that I reckoned that something terrible had happened to the *Verona*, because of the heavy sea and the fact that in my opinion if they could have got back they would already be here. 'It can't be as bad as that boy, go home and get your dinner and I'll have a look as I am going to the quay now,' said Dad. I went home to put the kettle on (Pat was over to the hospital at this time), I took my sea boots off and then I was that sure that something was wrong, I switched off the kettle and again put on my sea boots, and went off to the pier. On the way I met Dad and as we walked towards the quay and he caught sight of the sea I shall never forget him saying, 'My God boy, there is a sea.' When we got down the pier he immediately phoned one of the St. Agnes Pilots Jack Hicks, asking if he could see them but there was a rainsquall passing and so they said they would ring back. Dad now went to move the Steamship Company launch, leaving me to answer the phone. I then was so sure that I phoned the lifeboat secretary Mr. Moyle, telling him how I felt so he without hesitation told me to tell Dad to launch the lifeboat to go and see if we could find them. Very soon after Dad returned and at the same time the telephone rang, it was Jack Hicks to tell us that the squall of rain was passed, but they could see no sign of the *Verona*. We were soon away to search in the lifeboat. I already knew it was a hopeless task. We searched everywhere without any sign at all, but with the state of the sea that was running we knew that there was little chance of a boat of that type being able to survive. Also the fact that they would have most likely have been close around ledges, the boat would have been swamped with a single breaking sea. After returning that evening I had to pass Roy's door on my way home, and so had the terrible job of telling his mother, who had just lost her husband, and also Roy's wife, that there was no hope for them. Roy had been one of my mates ever since I could remember, we had always lived quite close to each other, our age was the same but for me being one day older, we were both fishing the same areas and at times I had gone with them in the *Verona* to do the lighthouse reliefs. I had also taken them in the *J.M.L.* on some occasions when their boat was out of commission for some reason or other; I would miss him in many ways.

The day after Roy was drowned Mr. Moyle met me in the street and said to me, 'If ever you feel like that again boy, don't worry about asking me, you get your father and launch the boat.' From that day on he did not ever question anything I did. Many times when the coastguard or anyone else had reported something wrong, if I could not get in touch with him by telephone, I would if I thought necessary launch the boat. Many times also after being out for several hours overnight, on our return I would ring him to say that we had been out and he would say something like, 'That's all right boy, I must have been sleeping on my good ear,' (he was deaf in the other). During all the time he was the Honorary Secretary I never once made out a service report, or ever saw one, he just put down what he thought, and then signed it for me.

I had a grin to myself one time, it was soon after the *Guy and Clare Hunter* had arrived, and he could not wait to send in my report on her behaviour during a bad weather exercise. I insisted on waiting for a really bad day, but also one when the direction of wind would allow us to re-house. When the right day arrived, we did the exercise. On return Mr. Moyle was waiting, 'Come in here a minute and we will do the report,' says he, but on giving it to me he also says, 'It's all right boy, I've filled it in, all you have to do is sign it.' He had answered all the questions about her performance during the tests, without even being aboard or seeing her behaviour, but that was the kind of thing one would expect from Mr. Moyle, and so I just signed it.

My brother Richard had now become bowman, and Roy Guy who was also fishing with his father, and was a schoolmate of mine and was two days younger, joined us in the lifeboat. I had also worked with Roy's father Algy when we were working under the Navy in the *J.M.L.* On the night of 21st January 1955 I was working in my fishing store and it was quite thick fog outside, also of course dark. I heard a steamboat blowing her fog signal and as it was getting very loud, I decided that as it was about nine o'clock I would pack up for the evening. The sound of a ship blowing at night in a thick fog is, I believe, the weirdest sound that one can ever hear. I then went into the shipwright's shop and told them of the ship I could hear, so we all went out to listen (they had not heard it as they had been using some power drills). After hearing it a few times, it stopped altogether, and I laughing remarked, 'Oh well, she has either gone away, or gone ashore, but I'm going home.' As I turned a corner on the way home I met the Bosun of the *Scillonian* Jimmy Jenkins from Bryher, and asked him if he knew if the *T.H.V. Stella* had arrived in the roadstead and dropped her anchor, accounting for the fog signal and sudden stop. Jim told me that the *Stella* was up at the Smalls Lightship, and so it could not be her. As we were talking my father passed, in a great hurry, I was back on to him but he said, 'Hello,' to Jim and passed us in a hurry. I called after him, 'Where are you going?' at which he turned back saying, 'I was looking for you, I've just had a call saying that there is a ship on the rocks 87 miles to the Westward, so you had better come home with me.' We both knew that it was impossible for a ship to be on the rocks in that position, as there were no rocks West of the Bishop. After we got home there was soon another message from Round Island lighthouse saying that it seemed as if there was a ship ashore on Men-a-vaur rock, they could not see anything for the fog, but were sure that's where it was. We soon launched the lifeboat and set off for Men-a-vaur, but it being low tide we now had to go around the back of Samson, through the North Western rocks, around the back of Bryher and Tresco to get there. This was not the easiest thing to do on a dark foggy night. On arrival we could see a fire, which they had lit on the after deck of a 7,176-ton vessel the *Mando*. She was hard aground on the Golden Ball rocks and we went straight alongside the Port side aft. They had lowered two lifeboats, had thrown in their kit bags etc. and were making fast a boats' rope ladder intending to board them. As there was quite a heavy swell, which makes a dangerous rise and fall, Dad told me to stop them, and so I went forward and two of our crew held me while I stood on the lifeboat's rails. When I got my chance I jumped for the ship's side and scrambled aboard. The Captain was on the afterdeck but was an Italian and I told him by motions that the crew must stop and bring the ladder to the stern where our men would take them off, otherwise someone was likely to get very badly hurt. As I was standing there with the Captain while the crew got off, I could feel the ship banging very heavily on the rocks under us, she was also hard on the rocks forward and would never get off again. As the crew were now on the lifeboat I asked the Captain if he had everything he needed, to which he indicated that he had and I then got aboard the lifeboat so that he may be the last to leave his ship. We now made for the entrance to Tresco Channel and when reaching there we met the island pilot gig *Sussex*, just coming out to look for the *Mando*. We stopped and told them that we had taken the crew off and as we were going into the channel, if they made fast one of the lifeboats we would tow them in with us. When we got in to Hangman's Island, a few hundred yards from Bryher, the ship's lifeboat's rope parted. After turning around to pick her up again, the Bryher men said it was all right as we were nearly there, and they would bring her in. We took all of the luggage out of the boat and left the ship's boat for them to take down to the customs house the next day, so we returned home.

The next day we went up to the *Mando* again in the Steamship launch, which Dad was skipper of, taking the Captain with us because he had left his logbook on board. There was too much swell to get aboard now, during the night it had washed a chained spare propeller, off the top of the house on her stern down onto the deck, and this must have weighed several tons. The next day we again went to get aboard if we could, also to salvage anything if possible. We again had the Captain with us in the *Kittern*, also two policemen and Mr. Ward who was the Steamship Company Chairman and Lloyds agent – this was not a very good selection for going salvaging.

We had no trouble this time and I among others jumped aboard. I made for the bridge first and found a pair of brass dividers, which I slipped into my pocket, and then went to where they had been working on the radar, which was out of commission, and the main cause of the stranding. Here on the deck was a new big chrome plated shifting spanner, and a nice ball hammer, both of

Mando.

these were too big to hide but I wondered how I could get past the watching eyes with them because these I considered as perks. I then stuck one in each sea boot, which were turned down to the knees length, so that the head of the hammer and jaws of the spanner were both showing. Now if the police or anyone said anything to me about them, I would say, 'It's no good coming to salvage without something like these,' and hope for the best. I now took off the brass steering wheel and then made for some of the cabins. Amongst other things I saw a 24-hour clock on the bulkhead, it was marked with the normal red 3-minute silence period on the hour and the half hour, which was the time when all ships would listen for an emergency message. The clock really was not very pretty at all but I thought it was nice as a keepsake, so I found a screwdriver in the drawer and took it off the wall. I can't remember what else I got which was for handing in to be sold for salvage purposes. When it came time to pack up and get back aboard I put the clock under my arm and got back aboard the *Kittern*. I just casually said that I had better put this in a safe place, and took it down in the cabin. I then stuck it under the flooring, right aft by the stern tube. On reaching St. Mary's we unloaded all the salvaged stuff, with my bits and pieces except the clock. After dark I retrieved this and took it home.

Some days later there were rumours that someone had stolen some personal gear including an expensive (I believe it was) gold watch, this was not the done thing. Most men would hand in any money or private belongings. The next thing was that some detectives arrived to try to find out who had taken the missing articles, including money. Pat was now worried about my clock, and so I told her I would get rid of it and off I went. I took it down to my fishing store and returned saying, 'It's gone.' The next day it starts again, 'Where did you dump that clock?' and not being able to lie to her, I admitted that it was in my store. 'Oh that's the first place they will look for salvage,' she says, so I then went down and took it out to our garden and put it in the chicken shed. Of course Pat again guessed that I still had it, and in the end she was so worried about this darned clock that I took it down the quay and threw it over the wall – so I still know where it is! As for the detectives, I think some of the missing stuff was found and two or three men appeared in court (locally), and the biggest laugh of the day was when the chief magistrate made his opening speech it ended with 'and so I think the less said about this, the better for everyone.' I can remember now the looks of amazement on the mainland reporters' faces, and the grins on the faces of the locals. We of course knew all the magistrates quite well and were killing ourselves with laughter inside, but even we were what one may call very surprised to hear his comment!

1955 was quite a busy year for myself, on the 22nd of July another ship struck the Seven Stones, she was the *Punta* of 2,197 tons loaded with phosphate rock, which was no good as a salvageable cargo. She was also registered in

Panama, the same as the *Mando*, which also carried a cargo of some type of coal, not salvageable. I was now fishing on my own and as it was foggy I did not know anything about it until I returned around midday, the lifeboat had been launched around 7.00 am and was still standing by the ship. I had a quick meal, made sure I had plenty of fuel and off I was bound to the Seven Stones again, this time in the *J.M.L.* I had a visitor passenger with me. On reaching the Seven Stones we found the *Cunard* now made fast to the stern of the *Punta*, with her crew now aboard the *Cunard* lifeboat. Made fast to her stern were two ship's lifeboats, the fog had lifted by now but was still hanging around and they were waiting for a French tug to arrive to see if there was any chance of salvaging the ship. We stayed until about four o'clock in the afternoon. My father had said that if and when we heard from the coastguard that they were returning with the crew, if I then came to meet them they would hand over the lifeboats to me and they would get home quicker and we could all have a bob or two as salvage.

I had not long been home when we heard that the lifeboat was going to return, but the Captain, his wife, and the three of his crew were staying aboard the tug *Abeille 26* until the next morning. This time Clifford Jenkins came with me, we met the lifeboat and as arranged took the boats in tow while they proceeded home with twenty of the ship's crew including two Somali stowaways, three cats, two linnets, a canary and a goldfinch. The next morning the fog closed in again, the *Abeille* had pulled the *Punta* off the rocks but she had broken in half and immediately sunk in deep water. They now required the lifeboat to bring ashore the Captain, his wife, and the rest of his crew, this we did with no great problem.

In December of 1955 I with Roy and Richard, and I think Harry went up to Cowes to bring home our new lifeboat. Henry Thomas was already at Cowes standing by the fitting out of the *Guy and Clare Hunter*. She was a little bigger, forty-six foot nine inches against the *Cunard's* forty-five feet, and a Watson designed boat. Instead of a small cockpit forward and a steering cockpit aft, she had an open steering position amidships which was half sheltered up to one's chest, with the two engineers positions and some crew's shelter under a metal canopy and a cabin behind the wheel, again about chest high. The engines were now diesel 60 hp Ferrys. The speed and range had not changed much with the *Guy and Clare Hunter* being a quarter of a knot faster at eight and three quarter knots, but if eased to seven knots there was a great improvement on the range. The engines were still controlled by wheels and levers, one engineer on each, and the coxswain's control was by word of mouth to the engineers sitting just in front and below him. We were still what we called a watch and compass job, except that I had asked for a direction finding ring be fitted, as it was in the bigger boats. After a bit of an argument and pointing out that there was a D/F station on Round Island, also that we were at times going off to sea over sixty miles on some occasions, with a very small area to find on the way home, especially in fog or poor weather, I now got the D/F fitted. This was something we had in the bigger Air Sea Rescue launches and so I knew how much of an advantage it could be.

It was late in December and the weather was really bad, we had our own engineer inspector also our South West Area inspector, and another that had just joined the R.N.L.I. He was a nice chap, and I remember on the trip down asking him what he did before this, to which he replied that he was in the Royal Navy. I offered to give him some good advice now that he was in the R.N.L.I., to which he replied that any advice would be welcome. So, I told him that the best advice I could give him was to forget he was ever in the Navy! I will remember that he gave me a big grin. I then explained that at that time all the men were fishermen, boatmen or men that had been to deep sea, and who knew their job better than any inspector. These men would not be messed about as they were all good boatmen, and a few gold rings on a uniform didn't mean a thing to them.

The first day out, as I have said was poor weather with force eight to ten winds all day. Within the first hour our own inspector was seasick and kept it up on and off all day. We went into Brixham that evening, and as I had never been into Brixham the inspector decided to take her in. When we got abeam of the entrance and there was no alteration, I enquired if we were still going into Brixham, to which I got the reply in a very naval voice, 'Of course we are.' As we were heading for Paignton I told him that although I had never been into Brixham I knew damn well it was not ahead, but now abeam of us, he was now very annoyed. At that moment Roy comes to the wheelhouse and says, 'I thought we were going into Brixham.' 'And so we are,' says the inspector, Roy then asks, 'Have they got any trains in Brixham?' 'Certainly not,' he replies. 'Well there's a bugger going in there now,' says Roy. It was getting dark and there was the train all lit up going along towards Paignton, at this there was a sharp turn to Port, a very sheepish inspector, and a delighted coxswain and crew.

We had the same weather the next day, but as we were going in towards Falmouth the wind started to ease off and so we suggested that we carry on to Scilly seeing that the weather forecast was very bad again for the next day, but if we carried on we would be home by midnight. This suggestion was turned down flat, and it was then said that if the weather was still as bad then we could stay in Falmouth until Friday, which was the 13th of December. In my opinion no self-respecting man would agree to take a new lifeboat to it's station and serve on her after arriving to start her service life on Friday the 13th! I told the inspector that no matter what the weather was we had to go, or if not I was finished with the job. We went into Falmouth and that night it blew 96 mph at the Lizard and in the morning the inspector did not want to set out for Scilly. I was really annoyed because I did like the job but was sure I would not stay in the boat unless we carried on. He then rang the Lizard coastguard station and asked what it was like in that area, the reply was that there was now the biggest sea they had seen for the winter. I then told him that I would ring my father and see what he said it was like. Dad said, 'It's not very nice boy, but it's good enough for you, you've got a lifeboat!' I knew that would be the answer and so I told Dad that the inspector wanted to call it off and so Dad must tell him that it was quite all right, which he did. We arrived in Scilly about 4 pm again soaking wet, cold but glad to be home.

Dad never actually took the *Guy and Clare Hunter* on a service trip as he was due to retire from the lifeboat. It seemed as if I would be asked to take over from him as coxswain by the crew and committee but there was a question as to who would be the 2nd coxswain, until one evening when I was working in my fishing store and Clifford Jenkins came in. It was no surprise to see him; he was a man that as kids we knew as Uncle Clifford because he had at one time worked with Dad and Uncle Jim in the fishing boats they had. He had also been in the lifeboat with them many years before and was not so much younger than my father. I had also worked with him as a rigger making rope ladders, cargo nets and fenders, he also used to come out fishing with me when he felt like a trip.

This particular evening after a minute or two I could tell that he had something he wanted to say. After a while he said, 'Well, what I've really come for is to ask for a job.' This really caught me unawares as I thought he wanted to come fishing with me and as the fishing was poor at the time I knew it would never pay, so I just said something like, 'Oh, what kind of a job then?' 'Well, I would like to come with you in the lifeboat when your father finishes.' I was surprised but very glad for him to take over and said so. He quickly said, 'Oh no, I don't mean as coxswain but as second with you.' 'Oh God, that's no good,' I told him, 'but I'll certainly be glad to go with you.' This then developed into quite an argument because I knew that he had been in the boat with both my father and grandfather, so how could I take charge ahead of him? In the end he said, 'Now look boy, I would like to go with you as 2nd coxswain but I told Trevelick that in no way will I take the boat, so you will have to make up your mind. Either I come as second or I don't come at all.' I could tell that he really meant it and I was delighted to have his experience to help me out when the time came. So Clifford joined us until he became of retirement age at 60, he then became a slip hand and my cousin Jim became 2nd coxswain. Jim was the winch man on the slip and had served many years in the Royal Navy until he returned home to work first as 2nd engineer on the *Scillonian*, then as engineer on one of the launches with Dad, then as skipper of the second launch. So history was now repeating itself with Matt as coxswain and Jim as second, both of these appointments were by a free and secret vote under the Inspector, which were afterwards found to be unanimous votes.

Clifford had been a good friend and a big help over the years. One time he was telling me a story of a time when he and my Uncle Alf, who had been drowned as a young man, had gone to Penzance for the weekend and they both bought a gold waistcoat pocket watch and chain. He then said, 'I will leave it to you when I'm gone.' This I took as a joke, but shortly after he died Carrie his wife called to me one day on the way to the boathouse. She gave me the watch saying, 'Here Matt, Clifford always said that this is to be yours.' It is of course something that I am very proud to have.

George Symons a shell fisherman then became winch man and afterwards a long and good member of the crew – like myself no matter what the weather was like he was always ready for a tin of soup on a long trip if it was possible to get it.

In the middle of May 1958 having done one or two services involving local boats there was some work to be done on the slipway and the boathouse. I did not see that it was necessary for the boat to go on a mooring in the harbour, and that it would be much safer to keep her outside the boathouse, on the slipway. This would not interfere with any of the work, which mainly concerned the winch engine. There was no problem to launch if we were needed, and if

R.N.L.B. 'Guy and Clare Hunter' ashore on Porth Mellon.

this happened, then we would have to put her on the mooring. After making it clear to Head Office that they would be responsible as I considered it was an unnecessary risk, I was told to moor her in the harbour as arranged. We moored her in the harbour on a good mooring with a new chain. During one night shortly after we had a very bad gale, where the wind again was in the mid nineties. The *J.M.L.* was on the beach moorings and at four o'clock in the morning started parting her mooring ropes. As she was close to the shore I managed to get aboard and then move her to the shelter of the old pier. My father had gone to the pier to help me moor up and after this was done and it was now breaking daylight I looked over the back of the quay wall to see if the *Kathleen* was all right, when I suddenly realised that the lifeboat was missing from her moorings. We rushed over to Porth Mellon and there she was, wallowing about on the beach, with the waves breaking over her, as she was well aground, side on and the tide ebbing. We had to wait until later to get aboard; on doing so found that she had broken the new chain about four feet outside the stem of the boat. She was undamaged having missed all the rocks except for a crack in her rudder, but she would still be serviceable until we could replace it. We laid a kedge anchor and tried to refloat her on the next tide, but were unable to and so the following day we arranged with a farmer to drag the sand away from close around her, because she had made a pit in which she was lying. We also dug a passage down the beach and with a lot of tackles from the anchor to her motor winch we floated her off. As the winch on the slipway was ready she was hauled up and the rest of the work carried out while she lay outside the boathouse as had been suggested. Not a word was mentioned about the stranding from Head Office, but I had a quiet grin to myself thinking, that will teach somebody up there something.

In 1958 we also had a new mechanic appointed, it was my Brother-in-Law Henry Taylor, who had been apprenticed to Henry Thomas, who was retiring (to later become the Managing Director of the Islands Steamship Company). Boy Henry as he was quite often called (just as I have always been known as Boy Matt even at the age of 78, this being due to the fact that we carried our father's names) was a first class mechanic and in fact too conscientious for the job as he later found. We were delighted to have Henry aboard, but I did wonder how he would cope in bad weather.

As it turned out his first service was to escort a damaged French trawler, which we chased all day. The Captain could speak no English, and so every message was passed back and forth between Brest Radio, Land's End Radio and us. This caused confusion and a great waste of time, also the trawler was changing course all the time, or reporting that he was now stopped and then a while after reporting he was under way again for Newlyn. After chasing him from the North West of the Islands we were to the North East of the Seven

Stones when we came across a big German cruise ship which was hove too, head to wind. I remember watching her forefoot coming out of the water, while the wireless operator was trying to find out if she had seen anything of the trawler. He reported in the negative and while this was happening Henry was checking our engines, so now we were shut down watertight again ready for off. As we cleared the shelter of the ship now at full speed again we hit a beauty and when we fell the stern of the boat must have hit before any other part as her bow tipped down and I fell forward onto the wheel. We had done a similar thing earlier in the day. Soon after a search aircraft that had also been looking for the trawler, flew over us and flashed us a message reporting the trawler ahead and to Port of us about five miles but when we met it we found that this was a Spaniard and not the French trawler. So, we altered course again to Starboard as I had expected. Soon after we received another message from Brest Radio, through Land's End saying that the trawler was now nearly at the Runnel Stone Buoy off Land's End. They now had an escort of another French trawler, and as he was still four or five miles ahead of us, was now being escorted, and because we would not catch them up before they reached shelter, we turned for home. I was a bit anxious about the course home as we had not seen any land all day, also it was again a watch and compass job, but I had kept a record on the chart and decided the course home would be South South West. After some while we again saw the aircraft and asked him for a bearing and distance to the Islands, he gave us West South West, but I considered that this was a mistake and carried on South South West. We then saw in the distance still hove to, the German ship and so requested his bearing and distance, which he gave as 22 miles North West. This was really ridiculous and I asked Henry to question it, but before he operated, I stopped him and then checked the chart, and as expected found that as I had guessed he was 22 miles North West of the Longships Lighthouse. As this agreed with my reckoning we carried on South South West making a sight of St. Martins on time and right ahead. I was quite pleased with this, as we had been chasing all over the place for about thirteen hours. Later on it was found that we had broken either five or seven big bolts in the bilge keels when falling heavily and during that day the wind speed was between 70–90 mph all day. A member of the Seven Stones Light vessel that I met shortly afterwards told me that they had just been fitted with a wave height measuring machine and that they had seen us passing, also that the height of the swell was measuring 60–65 feet and in the gusts when it would flatten the waves the swell was down to about 35 feet. As Henry had neither been sick nor sorry I was now very happy.

In 1959 amongst other things the coastguard reported flares being fired in the direction of the Bishop lighthouse one morning just before daylight. There was a gale blowing from the West, and just off Annet Head we found a tug the

Helen M. McAllister with an anchor chain out from the Starboard bow. On going close alongside we saw that there were several men all with life jackets on standing on the after deck. With our lights and the coming daylight we could see that this vessel seemed to be brand new. After shouting across to them to find out what was wrong we were told by the mate that they had lost all power, even for steering and had been drifting eastwards for 30 hours. They had lost one anchor after dropping both around the Bishop and the Captain who was on the bridge had told the mate that they were to abandon ship, and that he would jump overboard when she struck the rocks. I told him that he would not hit for a while and so we might save her if we got a launch to steer from astern, while we towed from ahead. We then put the 2nd coxswain Clifford Jenkins aboard, also my brother Harry telling them to lower the anchor chain to the

Helen M. McAllister.

next shackle ready for letting go as we could not raise it without power, while we returned to get a launch. When we returned Clifford told us that they could now use the hand steering and so after passing our tow rope they let go the anchor chain, which we now realised must have no anchor on it because they had by this time drifted about two and a half miles in less than thirty minutes and were not far off the Garrison rocks. After a bit of a struggle with the launch standing by we got her into harbour safe and sound.

These were the luckiest men alive, having drifted in a gale of wind for over thirty hours when they were fifty miles West of the Bishop with no radio power. They had drifted up between many ledges for six miles and only eventually finding some flares in one of the ship's life rafts, which the coastguards had seen, ended up safe and sound with no injuries and only the loss of two anchors and chains.

Another trip we had was to a submarine the *H.M.S. Trump*. It was fine weather but the Captain had reported a very badly injured man on board that needed hospital treatment so requested a Doctor and evacuation. We met the submarine and after the Doctor's inspection the man was brought aboard the lifeboat accompanied by the Commander to St. Mary's. The Commander was taken back to the submarine after seeing the man into hospital. The injured man was treated in our hospital, the Doctor saying that it was too dangerous to move him to the mainland. He finally made a full recovery and returned to the mainland.

Sometime in the late 1950's gig racing started again. I can remember the last gig race was in 1938 with many of the old Pilot gigs still around, and on August Bank Holiday there was always a water sports day. There are two or three of those old gigs still taking part in the racing of today. In those times there were swimming races as well as rowing and sculling and sailing races, then for a year or two there was a French fishing boat race. That started because the crab fishing boats worked around Scilly a lot and they got interested when they saw the other things that were happening. It was agreed to have a French crabbers race, sailing only, one or two by this time had a motor fitted, and the race became a big thing. One boat in the last race was beating the others hands down, until it was noticed that there was some grey smoke coming from under a bucket that was hanging on his side near the water line. He was made to stop the engine and she soon dropped back in the race!!

The war finished all that but in the late 1950's a local chap Noel Jenkins and the dentist Barry Fairest, with other helpers organised the Bank Holiday sports again. After maybe a couple or three years they were becoming very popular again and they thought it would be good to have a gig race from Nut Rock to St. Mary's as it used to be. Most of the gigs had both been bought by Newquay rowing club and refitted or they were past it and left to rot. There were two left on Bryher the *Czar* and the *Sussex*, and one on St. Agnes, which was an old cargo gig. After being asked by Barry and Noel if I could arrange a crew I asked one or two of the younger boat and fishermen who thought it would be great fun. We asked Mr. Jack Hicks and Dick Legg if we could have the *Campernell* to pull, they told us that she would not stand a chance against the other two, especially the *Czar* which was a lot lighter and more of a racing gig than the *Sussex*. They also wondered if we would be able to keep her afloat, but we were welcome to try.

We had the race which was a great success, won by the *Czar* and then the *Sussex*, and of course us a long way behind with myself steering and bailing like mad. We still had water halfway up between our ankles and our knees, and this started the real thing going again. The next year Barry and Noel approached Newquay's Mr. Gillis asking if they could borrow a couple of gigs. He agreed that St. Agnes could borrow the *Shah*, which was originally bought from St. Agnes if Mr. Jackie Hicks would agree to be responsible for her and the *Bonnet* could come to St. Mary's if I would be responsible for her. This was fine and after a couple of years, we tried again to buy the *Bonnet* back but ended up buying the *Golden Eagle*. I think the crew at that time was Roy Guy, Mike Hicks, Lew Hitchens, David Badcock, Les Green, Garfield Ellis and myself, we had a five pound share each and I think the only other was Doctor Bell. They then ran dances etc. to scrape up the rest of the money needed. After this, Newquay suggested bringing two gigs over every year for several years racing with ours, by this time there was practice as well taking place and it was taking up too much time for me and so I decided that my time had come to finish. There were new gigs built for the Islands and the mainland, and over many years things have progressed to enable us to host the World Pilot Gig Championships, races enjoyed by well over a thousand rowers and many many more supporters. I believe that there were eighty-five gigs on the starting line this year 2002.

It was around this time that we had a new lifeboat surveyor. When this chap arrived at the boathouse he introduced himself as John Chadwick. The name seemed to ring a bell to me, also his accent, so I asked him where he came from. He said that originally it was Flamborough but most of his early years were spent at Bridlington and his father had a fishing boat there but was now retired. He told me the name of the boat, I believe it was the *Mispha*, but it was certainly the name of a boat that I remembered. So it turned out that I had more than likely known his father and maybe even worked on his boat's engine with Ted when we were stationed there, and so we became great friends. Maybe it was because I did not give him too much work on repairs to the lifeboat over the years – in fact the only damage to any of the lifeboats that I had during my time was the smashed belting we suffered while taking off the crew of the *Torrey Canyon*, and a mast light when taking an injured man off a ship.

1961 was another big year for us, on June 22nd our second daughter Lucy was born and like Jean she was a lovely baby. We were delighted and Jean was now thrilled at having a sister. There was one big difference between them as babies, whereas Jean would sleep from 7 pm to 7 am Lucy did not seem to sleep for more than two hours at a time and it made very hard going when I was going to pots very early in the mornings and working sometimes until nine or ten at night.

I could always manage without much sleep and many times after getting up between 3.30 and 4 o'clock, working all day we would then get a call out in the lifeboat returning too late to bother about going to bed. I would just have something to eat and a cup of tea and go off to pots again, not going to bed until that night as normal. I never ever went to sleep while out in the lifeboat no matter how long it was. At one time when Lucy was a baby I didn't go to bed for three nights and two days working by day and sitting up with Lucy by night, and the third day was a Sunday. On Sundays I made a rule that I hauled my pots early in the morning as usual but did not work in the afternoon. Pat insisted that I went to bed after dinner which I did, but I was now for quite a while unable to get to sleep and after falling asleep awoke again at about 4 o'clock and got up for my tea.

When Jean was small we had a little Ford Eight motorcar so that we could go to see Pat's Mum and Dad with the kids on Sunday afternoon each week. Henry and Monica were now married and living close to us with their first daughter Julie, so there was Henry and I in the front and Pat and Monica in the back with Jean and Julie. In the end when they also had Sally and Andrew and we had Lucy we had to get a bigger car – it was still only a Ford Prefect but we all managed to squash into it somehow.

I had some very good years fishing around this time, as I was the only one left that fished around the Bishop and Crim area. The most I ever had in one string of eight pots was twenty two in the early morning and fifteen in the early afternoon when I decided to haul a few more before going home. This was mixed fish, mainly crayfish with a few lobsters in with them. The most I ever had was ten in one pot and I once shot a string of eight pots amongst the rocks for lobsters and the next morning when I hauled it I had twenty seven lobsters out of eight pots. Nowadays it seems impossible but I swear that these things are absolutely true, the prices in those days were low and one could buy a big cray for five shillings.

It was a job that gave a great deal of satisfaction most of the time. The fine summer mornings with the sun just coming up were better than any sunset but it was a job that became so much a way of life that even when things were not going so good, and I knew I could make a lot better living at other jobs, I still loved it being on my own having to make my own decisions and being answerable to nobody. There were many, many times when I was shivering with cold and wet through but it was all just part of it. I had many disappointments when after spending many of the winter days and evenings making new pots and splicing up new ropes, I would go out the morning after a gale to find that my gear was badly damaged or lost altogether.

I remember one time in particular when I lost so much gear that even though I used to allow an extra fifty per cent or more for losses, I still had to send to the mainland to get enough gear to carry on. When the Bishop lighthouse keepers came ashore on that particular occasion one of them told me that during that night they had heard a very worrying banging and scraping noise above all the other noise of the sea and wind. On going to the top gallery and shining a light down they found that it was the remains of one of my strings of pots hanging on a bracket above the kitchen window, 70 feet above

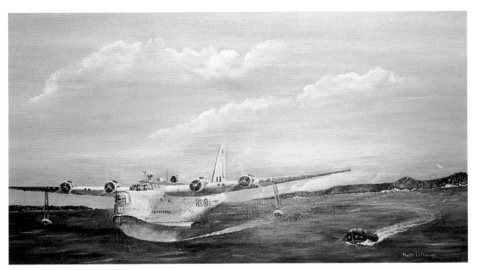

Painting of a Sunderland taking off from Scilly.

Painting of the 'Mando'.

Painting of the 'Ra Rau'.

Painting of the R.N.L.B. 'Robert Edgar' and yacht 'Concherto'.

Painting of the Seven Stones Lightship and T.H.V. 'Stella'.

Fishing the Western Rocks.

R.N.L.B. 'Guy and Clair Hunter' showing oil and damage after the Torrey Canyon service.

Models of R.A.F. Launches and Sunderland.

Family outing on the J.M.L. – left to right: Pat, Thomas, Lucy, Rebecca, Jean, Jemma and Myself.

Golden Wedding Day – left to right: Thomas, Jean, Myself, John, Jemma, Ken, Pat, Lucy, Rebecca.

sea level. It is incredible to think that the sea could have carried this up to such a height, as the weight of the gear must have been at least a couple of hundred weight. As a matter of interest, I had other things to think of when that was happening because at that time we were many miles North of the islands in the lifeboat! The noise they could hear was the stones in the pots and the metal buoys banging against the side of the lighthouse. They said that they had been quite worried until they found out what the noise was – I reckon I would have been quite worried just being there!

In 1962 we only did one service instead of at least three or four, but this does not mean that we did not launch because unless we actually rendered help of some kind, even if we searched for hours this did not count. The service was to take a sick man to Penzance for hospital treatment. Doctor Bell rang me sometime in the middle of the morning early in January to say that he had a patient that needed to get to Penzance hospital but as there was not much chance of any flying it being too foggy, could we take him and the patient over in the lifeboat. As this was quite normal procedure I agreed. He decided we should wait until one o'clock in case the fog lifted for flying, but as it was still thick when one o'clock came we left with them both for Penzance.

Doctor Bell was the only Doctor on the Islands so he wanted us to wait for him at Penzance so that he could return with us. I knew we would be coming home in the dark and possibly thick fog as well and so I decided to put the log out on the way over, as an insurance check on the way home – I believe this was only the second time we ever used the log. We made a good course and speed on the way over, the fog had lifted a little and we could just see the Wolf lighthouse, I checked the log abeam of the Wolf and again at the Runnel Stone. It must have been around six o'clock when we left Penzance for home with a visibility of four or five miles and so no problems. As we went out along the shore the Wolf Rock light which we had just sighted now disappeared again, and as we were going towards the Runnel Stone buoy light this also was disappearing but we now had the log out again and I checked the setting and so off we went with the fog getting thicker, also it was now dark. Checking my time and the log we should now be over to the Islands but could not see a thing, not even Peninnis Light or the red light of Round Island. I then remembered that I had used the Biggal of Menawethan as my starting point and so decided to keep on for another four or five minutes to make sure that we should be South of the Islands.

After we had run on for two or three minutes, Harry was standing in the wheelhouse doorway while I was at the wheel, he then remarked without thinking, 'It's calm here isn't it?' I thought, 'Yes, we must be in Crow Sound,' and asked Bill to shut both engines off to see if we could hear Round Island's fog signal. As I told Bill to shut off, so there was a shout from forward, 'Rocks ahead.' Luckily Bill had not had time to stop engines so we came full astern and stopped close to the rocks, now came the job of identifying the rocks. Searchlights are of little help as they just tend to reflect the glare from the fog, and a bunch of rocks all look the same. Because we had run our time and distance and had been in quiet water I decided unbelievable as it seemed we must be at Toll's Island and to prove this we would only have to steam South for a couple of minutes before seeing the half tide ledges. As it was about low water, if we did not find them then we must be somewhere else. As it turned out I was right and we had made a perfect landfall and so returned to the harbour feeling very very lucky.

1963 was a fairly quiet year for us with the lifeboat, we only did three services – one of these was another very lucky trip. It was I think in the late morning in June, again it was Doctor Bell, now the lifeboat secretary, who rang to say that a French trawler had a badly injured man aboard, they were heading for Newlyn and required a Doctor as soon as was possible. This message came from Brest Radio and on asking for a position I was told that all they knew was that the trawler had been fishing on the Sole Bank over sixty miles away from Scilly the evening before. They did not seem to be able to contact him, also he did not speak English and they did not know his course or speed. I said 'How in the devil are we supposed to find a boat that was in an area of the Lord knows how many square miles the evening before without having any information on his position, course, or speed.' Doctor Bell then said that they were sending a search aircraft out but the visibility was now very poor with quite thick drizzly fog, so I agreed to try.

I had decided it was the East Sole for some reason, I then guessed it would be one of the standard types of wood trawlers, which worked around here. I also thought that as the man was badly injured, the Captain would drive the boat at it's limit which in my opinion would be about nine and a half to ten knots. Now I began to think which side of the Islands would he go as it could be either, but if he went North of the Islands he would have the Islands themselves to cope with, also the Seven Stones, plus the Land's End area, and I then made up my mind that in this sort of visibility he would make to pass South of the Bishop about three miles. This would mean if he were short in his reckoning he would stand a chance of hearing the Bishop's fog signal. If he was on course or ahead of his reckoning he would be going farther clear of the Islands and rocks, also it would give him a clear run to Newlyn as long as he was South of the Islands. We went three miles South of the Bishop and turned onto the course I guessed that may be somewhere around the opposite to the one he would steer. After about two to two and a half hours, (I had just told Doctor Bell that I reckoned if we didn't see him within the next quarter of an hour we would have missed him) an aircraft flew over us on a reciprocal course, very, very low and on seeing us in the now really poor visibility, told us that he had now found the trawler about one and a half to two miles ahead of us. Within a short time we met him and put the Doctor aboard. Many times I have been told that I had had the luck of the devil, this was certainly one of them.

While thinking of luck, I think of the many times while I was fishing that my luck held good, I was being well watched over. One time, I was outside the Bishop on a dirty day with a couple of strings of pots aboard putting them in deep water for safety. As I was trying to get along outside of the deckhouse full of pots by walking side on, along the edge of the deck house leaning and catching hold of the pots, the boat made a big lurch which made me run forward. I went along the gunwale right to the stern board, in passing the Mizzen hoist I stuck my arm around it and instead of going straight over the stern I went along the stern board and back into the boat in a half circle. The luck of it was that this halyard had not been there the year before, and if it had not have been at this time, I would bound to have gone over the stern and would not now be writing of it. I had many close calls over the years and on many occasion my Uncle's words had nearly come true.

Another time I was trying to save my gear by shifting two strings of pots at the same time, the wind was on the starboard quarter and again it was far from nice weather. I was also trying to bait some of the pots as well as steer the boat, which was very stupid in the sort of weather it was. While bending over a pot I

Coming home from pots.

heard a noise and sensed something coming, I must have opened my mouth as all of a sudden I thought that I was under water. A sea had broken right over the quarter and side, as soon as it passed I found the boat half full of water and the platting that was the deck one walked on inside the boat was all floating around and the crayfish and lobsters were all swimming around inside the boat. Now I had a problem – I had a boat very heavy in the water and very likely to capsize or take in a lot more water, which I could not pump out because I needed to steer to keep the boat from being overwhelmed or broaching too. I steered downwind towards a rocky island until in the shelter of it and then it took me about two hours to bail with a bucket and pump out the water and sort things out so that the boat was now safe again.

On at least three occasions I have had my foot up on the rousing ready to jump overboard. At times a heavy sea running in between ledges or when doing something to save time in bad weather, I have been caught thinking that the boat was going to turn right over, but she was a beauty. When all seemed lost she would dig the skeg in, lift her bow and run like as if the devil was chasing her, as straight as a die.

We had the usual three of four services during 1964 one of which involved myself in the *J.M.L.* on the way to pots one morning just breaking daylight. I saw a flare just off Peninnis Head, I started my second engine and lit a diesel soaked rag in a bucket to try to warn anyone that there was someone in trouble and carried on towards the flare at full speed. About quarter of a mile off the rocks I could see a white boat which turned out to be an ex-R.N.L.I. forty-five foot lifeboat, now converted to a yacht called the *Waratah*, with two men on board. She was very low in the water and was sinking. I had a towrope ready and asked them to come aboard with me. They refused, but requested me to tow them into the beach about three quarters of a mile away. I did not stop to argue but started towing as hard as I could. As we were getting closer the *Waratah* was getting lower in the water and when a few hundred yards away, I was very doubtful if she would stay afloat long enough to make the beach. I kept towing until I just had enough room to let go the tow and turn away to avoid running ashore myself, whilst the *Waratah* had sunk to her gunwale level as she hit the beach. The owner who was partly crippled now realised that he was very lucky as he was unable to swim. At this time the lifeboat came into Porthcressa and later that day I returned in the lifeboat with a pump. After she had been patched we towed her off and took her into the harbour.

It was around this time that the Islands' Steamship Company had a new vessel called the *Queen of the Isles*, so for a few days several of our crew were off the islands on holiday or were at the christening of the new ship. Included in those absent were the honorary secretary, the first mechanic, the chairman and

Waratah and J.M.L.

the deputy honorary secretary. As I was walking up the road one evening I met
the deputy chairman of the lifeboat committee and he seemed to be in a bit of
a state. 'What is going to happen if the lifeboat is wanted?' he asked. 'I don't
know what you mean,' I reply. 'Well, half of the crew including the launching
authority is on the mainland, who is going to launch it?' I told him that I had
the authority to launch the boat at any time if I thought it necessary, even if
they were all here and I would be answerable to the R.N.L.I. for my action. As I
had plenty of spare men that would go with me there was no problem. 'This
state of affairs is not good enough,' says he, 'Do you realise that we have not
had a committee meeting for at least three years?' I replied, 'Well, Mr. …, if
there has been no need to call a meeting for at least three years, surely you
should consider yourselves very lucky and if you can find me another station
around the coast with the same troubles I would like you to let me know where
it is!' – and so ended that little chat.

1965 I was phoned by Doctor Bell saying that there was an injured man on
Round Island Lighthouse, who needed to get to hospital on St. Mary's as
quickly as possible. The tide was quite low and still ebbing but I took a chance
and went up Old Grimsby Channel. As it was dark and we could get stuck on
the way up I had my fingers crossed, but after touching the bottom a couple or
three times we got through to Round Island where we stuck our bow in close
enough for the Doctor to jump ashore. After about three quarters of an hour

he returned with the other two keepers carrying the injured keeper in the stretcher. As the wind was about force seven blowing straight onto the little landing area, which was not big enough for us to get alongside, we had him swung out on a small crane, and after getting him aboard we took off the Doctor. When he came aboard I told him that we could no longer get down the shorter channel but would have to go around Tresco and Bryher and then down through the Northern rocks. His reply I shall always remember, 'Matt, you can go which way you like now, I've done all I can and so it makes no difference'. Happily the keeper survived O.K. and after some time returned to duty, as far as I know.

Soon after this the *Guy and Clare Hunter* went away for refit and the fitting of a radar set, which was paid for by a visitor friend of ours. This was the first radar to be fitted to a lifeboat. After many trips finding our way around the rocks, or back into the islands from over sixty miles away, sometimes also in fog as well as a dark night or gale of wind, I was in clover. Because of the scanner height, we could often in really bad weather only be sure to pick up the islands about seven or eight miles away. If we were looking for trawlers etc. we would pick them up only as far as one and a half miles away, but compared with before having the radar, it was a piece of cake.

As a relief boat while the refit was taking place we had our old lifeboat the *Cunard* and so we were quite at home in her and during her stay we towed in another yacht called the *Sea Ranger*.

Towards the end of the year 1965 we now had the *Guy and Clare* back, I remember we had some really hard gales and during this time we were called out to meet a ship which had found a twelve metre racing yacht of former days, which was disabled and unable to steer. This ship had taken her in tow but was having trouble actually towing the yacht. The ship had asked for us to relieve him but he did not want to come closer than twenty miles from the Islands. There was a very heavy sea running, the wind had moderated to about a moderate gale, but the forecast gave it to back around to the South East and freshen to force ten again by evening. Owing to this I told my Father, who was the head launcher not to worry if we were late getting home, and that I was going out past the Bishop way to judge the amount of sea. Then if I considered it necessary, I would go up around the islands to Tresco Channel and await the tide and daylight. We met the ship, which quickly dropped the tow and was gone. We connected up with about one hundred fathoms of nylon and a weight in the middle to ease the spring and snatching on the way home. I had to keep using the throttles all the time, altering from full speed to try and keep ahead of the *Barranquilla* (as she was called), which should have been towing astern. At times she would come charging up until she was ahead or abreast of us and on two occasions I looked aft to see Rodney and Richard with their hands on her stem trying to push her bow one side of our stern. It was a bit of a worry towing her up Broad Sound, especially between Jeffrey Rock and the Old Wreck buoy, as I was afraid to get too close to the ledges. Also, if I didn't get it right we would end up one side of the buoy with the *Barranquilla* on the other side and she would then have the ledges breaking on her. The wind had already gone around to the South East and had freshened into a moderate gale again. I was thinking how glad I was that I had come in that way, because on the way home it was suggested that we go in for St. Mary's Sound, as it would be an easier passage. I had not agreed however, and as I was Boss there were no arguments. As we were crossing the entrance to St. Mary's Sound a chap said, 'My God it's piping out there now, it's taking up the water,' and so I was delighted to just say, 'Yes a good job we aren't down there South of St. Agnes now with this lot behind us.'

Pot making.

We came into the pier and my Dad was lying flat on the pier shining a torch on the corner because he was afraid of being blown overboard.

I think that by this time I had decided that it was of more gain for me to spend my winter months trawling and making my own pots, rather than working on the launches, and making as many pots as I could in the evenings. Over the years I had in some of the winter months worked on the launch with Dad as an extra hand to cope with the flower season and the bad weather, also as skipper if he was ill or on holiday.

I well remember one bad day we went to St. Agnes on the higher water, so that we could use the *Kittern*, a 52 feet ex-navy launch at the short quay. The quay that we used on the high water was not very much longer than the launch and at the shore end it curved up to the cobbled road. The St. Agnes men shouted out to us that it was not fit to try to load the flower boxes, but as there were not many, Dad decided that we could and went alongside. The mail and flowers were being quickly loaded when a spell of extra big sea came in and when the sea ran back the *Kittern* was aground on her keel and falling over onto her bilge. The next thing we knew she parted her stern rope and went forward with the sea until she hit the bottom on the way up the start of the roadway and then fell on her side again when the sea ran back. When the next sea came in the engine was already going full astern and so lucky for us we came off again and returned to St. Mary's with the flowers and mail.

Another time some years after, I was crewing with Dad and again at St. Agnes but by now there was a new quay. On the higher waters the end would be under water and as there was no back wall, it was a job to get alongside, or sometimes to get away from in bad weather. On this particular day, the run of the sea dragged us in to the corner and we knocked a hole in the bow. As she was now leaking badly as soon as we got to St. Mary's she was put on the beach and Dad told the manager that we would have to take the *Tean*, another ex-navy boat roughly the same pattern but with a higher bulwarks and not the same to handle. The manager says, 'But she has not done her trials yet,' she had just been fitted out and re-engined but my father says, 'Oh well, this will do for her trials as we have to get the St. Martins' flowers and mail.' We got into St. Martins with the end of the quay being under water and loaded everything aboard. We came astern and when far enough, turned hard to Port expecting to turn out clear of the pier end, but the wind was on the Port side and the *Tean* did not turn as well as the *Kittern*. Dad went astern again nearly onto the beach, then full ahead hard to Port again and we went out over the top of the pier bumping the keel twice on the way. This time luckily there was no damage.

I liked trawling but it was heavy work hauling and so I put in a new mast step and mast clamp in front of the after engine house, so that I could shift the mast from aft to amidships. This was a great improvement because I could now tow from amidships, shoot the trawl boards on both sides while on a straight course and by the use of snatch blocks could haul the trawl aboard by using the capstan with no trouble. Many times when I was trawling, on their way back to St. Martins in the Steamship Launch, the people would ask Dad to come out to me when I was working in Crow Sound to get some fish. In those days it was five good plaice for two shillings and if I was having a good day, I would know when he would be on his way and go in to meet him to make sure that I would get rid of a lot of my day's catch before returning to St. Mary's. (What the eyes don't see the heart doesn't grieve over).

1968 again was the usual four or five services; one was to a ship that had a bad list, caused by a cargo shift due to the very bad weather. The Penlee boat had been escorting her during the night and we were asked to relieve her. The *Firth Fisher* as she was called, was unable to risk turning so that she may get shelter, so we relieved the Penlee boat about ten or twelve miles South of the Bishop. We then escorted her slowly along heading into the North West gale. A submarine arrived to stand by and after about three quarters of an hour a big bulk carrier also arrived, the *Scillonian* at about the same time. The then captain of the *Scillonian* wanted me to advise the *Firth Fisher* to turn towards Scilly for shelter and to right his cargo. I considered it was too risky, so I replied that I would not and that I considered that the *Firth Fisher's* master knew what he was doing and it was entirely up to him – he knew his ship best. The *Scillonian* then asked the bulk carrier Captain if he thought she should make for Scilly. I was delighted to hear the Captain of the bulk carrier (a really big ship who must have been listening) answer by saying, 'If you think so, I suggest you tell him yourself'. He then asked the *Firth Fisher* if it would benefit him if he turned slowly to the starboard that would give the much smaller *Firth Fisher* a chance to turn while under the shelter of his lee side. This was gladly accepted and was successful; he then set off for the Lizard with us as escort. When we were South of Newlyn the submarine, which had left us at the Scillies, told him that he had gone around the Lizard and that the weather was much better than expected. The *Firth Fisher* was happy to proceed alone and so we returned home, later receiving a nice letter of thanks from the Captain and owners.

We also took the crew of six off a French trawler the *Petit Jean Yves* that ran ashore one evening in January. It was about eight o' clock when she ran onto the rocky shore on the South side of the island of Gugh, she was very lucky to hit a place where the rocks were reasonably flat but sloping towards the sea. However, there was a strong South East wind blowing right on shore and she went on the rocks at full speed. When we got to her she was well aground with her bow and a good part of her keel showing, it was obvious that she would not be got off at that time. As the crew were all aft with their belongings, we managed to stick our bow in far enough for them to get aboard us and get away again without any damage. The next morning the wind had changed direction and moderated and so on the high water we took the crew back to their boat. We laid out an anchor astern of him and with us in the lifeboat pulling at full speed and his engine also going astern, plus him pulling as hard as he could on the wire to the anchor with his trawl winch, we re-floated him. After a bottom inspection it was found that she was not too badly damaged and she went on her way.

Also that year Bill, Roy and myself went to London to be presented with our medals for the service to the *Braemar*. Pat, Jean and Lucy came with me, while

Roy and Bill's wives accompanied them. Doctor and Mrs Bell came; the Chairman of the Council was also coming but for some reason that I can't remember, was unable to in the end. Princess Marina presented us the medals, and after the presentation we were invited to have a cup of tea and a chat with her. It was a bit special for me as Princess Marina had presented Dad with his Bronze medal for rescuing twenty-five men from the *Mando* in 1955. Very sadly our presentations were the last she made before she died. We had been invited to visit No. 10 Downing Street and were warmly welcomed by the then Prime Minister and his wife (Mr. and Mrs. Wilson to us), as they had been visitors to the Islands for many years and now had their own bungalow on St. Mary's. We were shown around the Cabinet room etc. until the Prime Minister was called away, and Mrs. Wilson invited us up the famous staircase with the pictures of previous Prime Ministers lining the walls. We went into their private flat where we had some tea and chatted about the local news in Scilly. We had a great laugh as we left; when we had entered the street it was empty except for about two people, now it was crowded with people and reporters, wondering who these important people were – they must have had a great disappointment on seeing us!

We had three or four services in February 1970; I remember one of them again was to a ship with a shifted cargo, again North of Round Island. On this particular occasion the message from the coastguard was that a Dutch ship had a list of 30 degrees and required assistance, he also wanted to try and get the shelter of the Scillies, which were only fourteen to fifteen miles away.

There was a visiting Inspector here at the time and so I contacted him. He was with the Honorary Secretary, (Doctor Bell had finished by this time), and anyway the Inspector told me that we should not launch the boat as he considered that the Dutch vessel only needed a Pilot. I then pointed out that Roy and myself were the only ones with a Trinity House Pilot's Licence; also in that sort of weather (a moderate gale with heavy swell) there was no other way that we could get to help him. He still said that we were not to launch.

I was really annoyed to hear such a stupid statement and returned home to speak to the coastguard. As I got inside my door the telephone was ringing, it was the coastguard who informed me that there had been another message from the ship saying that their list was increasing and he was asking for any ship in the area to stand by him. On hearing this I told the coastguard to inform him that we were on our way. I then went back to the Inspector saying, 'We have to go now as the ship's list is increasing, and he is asking for any ship to stand by him.' I was astonished and flaming mad when I was told that we could not launch, and so I just told him that I didn't care a damn what he did, but I was taking the boat (which I was within my right to do) and that he could come with us if he liked, or he could stay there and I would argue with him when we returned. I then walked out and made my way to the lifeboat house.

I had already asked Pat to phone the crew and so on my arrival we were almost ready to go. In a few minutes we were ready and I had just told them to push the ladder back, when the Inspector arrived in the doorway. On seeing him I told them to hang on, to give him chance to come if he wanted to. He came aboard and I shouted to let go, so off we went. There was not one word passed between us until we sighted the vessel ahead of us. She was rolling heavily to Port and I shall never forget the Inspector's remark on sighting her, 'Oh my goodness, she has got a list!' I will not tell what my remarks were but they were not very complimentary! The most amusing thing was that when I saw the service report, it said that on the morning of the 24th of November 'it was decided' to launch the St. Mary's lifeboat, and continued to state the reason for the launch etc. It was obviously thought unnecessary to name the person responsible for the launch! We had of course brought the vessel into St. Mary's where some of her cargo was re-stowed by the crew and local stevedores, and a couple of days after they went happily and I expect very thankfully on their way.

On the 15th of July Dad passed away while he was lying on the sofa reading, and then dropping off to sleep. Although it was such a loss, I was afterwards pleased that it had happened that way.

Many years before, after I had been fitting out the *Kathleen* for him every year so that he need only to jump aboard and go sailing each summer, I was painting her when another local man remarked something about selling her. Dad then said, 'She will never be sold in my time, but I don't know what will happen when I'm gone.' I then told him not to worry and that she would not be sold out of the family while I was alive. He had told me before, 'When anything happens to me boy, she is your boat don't forget.'

Just before he died he told me that he would not be going sailing that year as it was getting a bit much. Two days later he was saying what lovely weather it was and so I knew what he meant and said that if he wanted the boat rigged she was all ready except for shipping the masts (by crane) and so we would do that when I returned from fishing the next day. The next day it was not such a nice day, so when I went to get him to ship the masts he had said that as the weather was not very nice we would do it tomorrow. He was a very happy man thinking of going out sailing again in the boat that he had spent a great deal of his life in, and it was the same afternoon when I was called because he couldn't be awakened for his tea.

Dad's funeral, I would say was the biggest ever seen in Scilly. Many from the mainland, who also attended, knew him. He could be very awkward at times, but although he was rough on the outside, he was very gentle on the inside. His word was his bond and no arguments.

Before I go on, I remember one night in particular it was blowing 85 mph at the coastguard tower, and the Honorary Secretary Mr. Moyle rang to tell me that St. Agnes had reported flashes of light thought to be around the area of a ledge of rocks, just a short distance off the Western shore. I answered saying that I would call the crew and we would go and look. He said, 'No hang on a minute boy, it's a terrible night, and an awful place to get at, also they are not flares but just flashing lights.' I then told him that if it were something in trouble the sooner we went the better for us, as we would be unable to help if she went ashore in that area on a night like that. It was agreed that I would ring him from the boathouse before we left. When I got to the boathouse I rang Mr. Moyle and he then told me that it was worse than ever as the lights were now suspected to be at the back of the Brows. These are a line of ledges and rocks with no shelter at all from that particular direction of wind and sea, therefore he was not keen on us launching. I gave the same argument as before and told him that I would rather go now; he gave in telling me to take care. Dad was as usual on the slip, looking quite concerned he looked up and says, 'You watch what your doing tonight down there boy.' I knew he would have been of the same opinion as I was and so off we went.

It was before the radar days and we had to make some dog's leg alteration of course without any guides at all. We did see St. Agnes trying to flash us for about a minute between squalls of tipping rain but in truth from the wheelhouse all I could see was the bow of the boat, sea and spray reflected in the steering lights and nothing else. Reckoning how long it would take to travel in between each change of course I made the necessary alterations. We were now in my reckoning about half way, when we saw the Bishop flashing for half a minute during a break in the rain. A short time after we saw this again just for a few flashes, eventually we were getting close to the lines of rocks and the Brows according to any timing. We had been driving at full speed so that I could judge the distance covered better. I was now thinking of easing down, as I was sure that we were very close, when we received a message calling us back to station. I now had to reverse the procedure but could not reverse course because of tide allowance. So all was done by guesswork and by God, but each time knowing that we must be right so far until we were off the Newman Rock and could just see the loom of lights from St. Mary's. I knew Dad was worried and so we set off a flare to let them know we were back. When we got the boat back in the house, I asked him if he had seen our flare less than half a mile away, they had all been watching for us but saw nothing. Jim, my first cousin, who at the time was 2nd coxswain, told me after that my Father had beckoned to him on the boat before we launched to say, 'Keep an eye on him tonight for God's sake, and don't let him take too many chances.'

As it turned out they had found the cause of the flashes – it was a wind operated electric dynamo shorting out, which was on a pole in line with the areas they had considered to be the rocks. This although it would not be recorded was certainly the darkest and possibly one of the luckiest nights we had – just to get there and back without seeing anything or getting into serious trouble. There were many dirty trips, not quite as worrying as that one, but as these were counted as 'no service' they were not recorded and are now in the past and forgotten.

Dad was awarded the B.E.M. in the New Years Honours list for his work for more than thirty years as coxswain of the lifeboat, but sadly he did not live to receive it. My brother Harry did this on his behalf. Dad over the years had also been awarded a Silver medal from the R.N.L.I., also one from the Italian Government for his part in the rescue of the men from the *Isabo*, and there was a vellum signed by Mussolini. He was awarded the Bronze medal for the rescue of the crew of the *Mando* and a vellum for rescuing the crew of the *Jonas Lie*.

During 1971 we did one service in the *Guy and Clare Hunter*, which was to take a sick man off a motor vessel. The *Guy and Clare* then went for refit.

The first service we did in the relief lifeboat the *Jessie Lumb* was to an Australian yacht the *Koomooloo*. It was quite a long service in poor weather; her position was given to be about forty-two miles North West of the Bishop Light. I believe she had lost her rudder and had given out a May Day call; the main trouble now would be for us to find her. Yacht's positions in those days were usually not very accurate, they were mostly dead reckoning positions, also the yacht was now drifting with the weather and it was going to take us about five hours to get there to begin our search. After we had just cleared the islands we were told that the tug *Utrecht* had left Mount's Bay and was also going to her assistance. On hearing this it was immediately said that as she could do sixteen knots she would be there long before us. When they realised that we were a little more than half her speed, but already less than half their distance from the position, plus the fact that yachts were very rarely where they thought they were it was plain that we had a good chance of being first on the scene. Also until she was found, it was our job to search for her. When we reached a position about eight miles away from her as we thought, we had a call from a merchant ship saying that he was at her position but could see no sign of the yacht. He then asked her to fire a rocket, I told those on deck to watch all around the boat when we suddenly saw it shoot up right abeam of us. We were soon in sight of him, and we could also see the merchant ship coming up from the West. When we got close alongside the yacht he asked us to stand by because he had already made a salvage agreement with the tug to tow him into Falmouth. After an hour or so the tug arrived and we offered to pass his line for him but he declined. After a couple or three attempts he asked us to do it for him, and when he was made fast he then asked if we would escort them for a while until he was happy with things. We did that for about one and a half hours until the tug released us, we were then glad to open the throttles again on course for home.

Some time later I had a letter from the owner of the *Koomooloo*, thanking us for our help, also saying that he had called for the tug because he did not realise that lifeboats operated so far from their stations. There was also a cheque for fifty pounds for us to take our wives out for the evening, this we did. It turned out to be such a good evening that every year afterwards we had a lifeboat party, it was so popular that we could not accommodate all those that wanted tickets to attend.

There were three or four more services before the yacht *Moronel* gave out a May Day call, giving her position to be thirteen miles South of the Bishop Rock Lighthouse. She reported that both masts and her bowsprit were broken and most of her rigging lost. There were two men on board, one of which was very ill with seasickness. We set off for the reported position in a moderate gale from the North East and quite a heavy sea. About one and a half hours later we were given a new position, ten miles South of the Wolf Rock and so we altered course. Shortly after this we were told that a Russian ship had found her and was attempting to take her in tow. They were unsuccessful and so carried on their way.

As we got nearer to the position we asked the yacht to fire some rockets and by this means found her fifteen miles South East of St. Mary's. We got close alongside at 12.30 pm, the wind having now changed to a North Easterly force nine. We passed a tow and started for home, before long the tow parted as we thought, but what had happened was that the yacht's bollard had been pulled out of the deck. I knew then that we would need to put one of our crew aboard to rig the tow. Rodney said he was willing to go and so I put the lifeboat quarter close to her bow and he jumped across. A bridle was rigged and the tow passed, the chain bridle parted soon after. We connected up again this time with a single length of her anchor chain. At 3.40 the tow again parted and was re-connected. We set off at about two knots, again at 5.40 she parted and was re-connected. At about 6.30 our starboard engine stopped, after a while it was started again and we carried on slowly and arrived home at about a quarter to eleven that night. We afterwards found that one of her headsails was hanging underneath her with part of her bowsprit and mast; this was acting as a drag causing all the trouble. Rodney and myself were given vellums for this service.

'Moronel' and lifeboat back in St. Mary's.

Soon after this we had the *Guy and Clare Hunter* back from refit – she had now been re-engined with two Ford Mermaid engines, which were much lighter and a lot more powerful. It made her a much better boat; she was still the worst boat that I had ever handled in my life, but safety wise I never ever doubted that she would get us back.

We did five more run of the mill services in 1972 making a total of eight for the year. We had a quiet year in 1973 but did have one run, again to the Seven Stones, as it was reasonable weather there was not a lot to it. Nevertheless we delivered some fresh newspapers and magazines which was the normal procedure if we were passing on a non-service trip, but in this case we were going to take off a sick man from the lightship and he was brought ashore for treatment.

We were quite busy again in 1974 with landing sick or injured men, or towing in yachts etc. Sometimes these services (classed as 'gave help') could mean that we had had a really nasty trip such as the 'St. Agnes lights', many of which would be called non-service. One service I remember to a yacht, we had a bit of a job to find her because of the weather and poor position, there were also two Dutch rescue tugs looking for her, one was the *Utrecht*. Eventually we found her by shining our searchlight skywards, which could be seen quite a long way at times. We then took her in tow reporting to Land's End Radio that we now had the yacht in tow and were returning to station. This was not a very nice night at all. When I reported to Land's End the *Utrecht* called the other tug asking, 'Had he heard our message?' The *Zwart Zee*, I believe it was, replied that he had not and so the *Utrecht* then told him to go over to the frequency of 1552. On hearing this I was interested and tuned to 1552. The *Utrecht* then said, 'A message from the St. Mary's Lifeboat says that they have the yacht in tow and are returning to St. Mary's, so we might as well go home, because they are in bloody good hands now.' This from men like a salvage tug skipper was praise indeed for all of us.

Another good example of searching was the service to look for the *Fair Judgement*. Dr. Bell, Roy and myself were all aboard the *S.S. Kungsholme*, which was anchored in Crow Sound . At about 17.30 a message was received by radio to inform us that the yacht *Fair Judgement*, which was on passage from Gibraltar was in difficulties by his reckoning a distance of 12 miles to the South of the islands. She had encountered bad weather since leaving Gibraltar, the crew were exhausted, they were short of food and they didn't think that they could endure another night at sea. They had not originally intended to call at Scilly and didn't have the necessary charts, so they were requesting the lifeboat to escort them into St. Mary's, their E.T.A. at Peninnis Head being approximately 18.30–19.00.

We were taken ashore by Laurie Terry in the *Soleil D'Or*. Harry was also at the *Kungsholme* in the *Gugh* and Richard was there in the *Golden Spray* and so they also returned to St. Mary's. The lifeboat was out on the slipway ready for launching, after speaking to the coastguard it was decided to launch right away and to meet the yacht in daylight if possible.

On reaching position at Peninnis Head the yacht was not in sight and so we steered South to meet her. When about seven miles off we managed to contact her by wireless. We asked what their position was but they could not give us one but still thought they were a few miles South of the islands. We tried to get a wireless bearing but the signal was poor and so we could not get one that was dependable. We then asked her if she could see any lighthouse lights as these were now lit and visibility was good. She replied that she could not and so we decided to let off a flare. As she could not see the flare or the lighthouses we decided that at the time she could not be within twenty miles of the islands and so we returned to St. Mary's to wait until she was closer.

On reaching the slipway St. Agnes reported lights South of their lookout, which we considered to be a ship that we had seen passing from East to West as we returned. To make sure however, we again went out through St. Mary's Sound. On reaching the Spanish Buoy a message was received from Land's End Radio stating that the yacht did not know where she was but they could now see a treble flashing light, they were steering 135 degrees with the light right astern. It was therefore thought that she must be around the Seven Stones as that was the only light giving three flashes in our area and so we altered course towards the Stones.

Shortly after altering course for the Seven Stones, Land's End received another message from the *Fair Judgement*, which we intercepted stating that as they seemed to be running into shallow and breaking water they had now again turned to a northerly course. This all seemed wrong because if she had been steering 135 degrees with the Seven Stones light astern, she could not possibly be getting into shallow water. Also as the visibility was very good she should see the Wolf Rock light ahead of her, Round Island on her starboard quarter and the Longships and Pendeen to port. The wind was West to North West about force 6–7 with quite a bit of western sea. We were now just passing the Eastern Islands, so continued towards the Seven Stones.

At the time I began to wonder if they had mistaken two flashes for three. If this were so, then it did make some sense as regards to running into breaking water etc, as this could mean they would be around the Bishop Rock lighthouse. The situation was made more worrying by the fact that neither Land's End Radio or ourselves could get any reply from our radio calls for the rest of the night. To complicate matters more after the *Kungsholme* had left Scilly for the Bristol Channel she reported sighting a yacht of her description off Hartland Point at approximately 23.00, but it did not seem possible that this could be the *Fair Judgement* so we continued searching around the Stones expecting to possibly find some wreckage.

During the night we extended our search to the East and North, the wind now being about South West Force 7. We spoke to a ship about six or seven miles North West of the Longships light which had been keeping a lookout as requested by Land's End, but she had seen no sign of the yacht or wreckage.

At about 09.30 the next morning we were North East of the Seven Stones when much to both our own and to Land's Ends' amazement the *Fair Judgement* came up loud and clear on the radio stating that he was now in sight of a French fishing vessel but had no idea where he was. He was told in no uncertain terms to ask the fishing vessel to report his position. This was done and the position turned out to be around the Smalls Rocks off the coast of WALES! This made everything fit it, breaking water, the whole lot.

So we had spent all night searching for a yacht, which must have been about one hundred miles away. We returned to St. Mary's somewhere around midday. A helicopter dropped an experienced yachtsman aboard her to guide them to Milford Haven. He also I believe managed to lose himself for a while but eventually with more help the *Fair Judgement* was berthed at Milford safe and sound – much to the relief of the Land's End Radio operators, no doubt!

1975 was again a normal five-service year of fishing boats, yachts and sick or injured men. I was also awarded the British Empire Medal in the New Years Honours list. Neither Pat nor I was looking forward to going to London. At this time we had a visit from a big German lifeboat with her crew and a couple of officials from their lifeboat service, to have a service to commemorate the loss of over three hundred lives and the saving of twenty five from the wreck of the Hamburg Americas line ship *Schiller* one hundred years before. I was then asked if I would have the medal presented in the Town Hall by the Lord Lieutenant of Cornwall (the Queens representative, Sir John Carew Pole), this was fine by me! As the American Ambassador, the German Ambassador and the French Naval Attaché and some others had come for the service, they and our own Lady Mary Wilson who was for many years the Chairwoman of our Ladies Lifeboat Guild, were with many locals who attended the presentation. We then attended a lunch at the Godolphin Hotel where Pat and myself were sat one each side of Sir John. He turned out to be a great laugh, wanting to know about all those present and he certainly knew all that went on in the real world (outside the dinner parties and social functions). After the lunch I had the pleasure of taking the German lifeboat as Coxswain down to the Bishop area where the *Schiller* had been wrecked. I had fished this area for many years and had often had my pots caught fast in her rusting plates or pulled up rusty lobsters, so I knew exactly where her remains were. We stopped right over the remains where the local clergy carried out a service, and the representatives of the different countries laid their wreaths. We then went around some of the rocks, the German lifeboat official was getting quite worried about being in amongst the rocks so close and kept suggesting that I might let someone else steer and he would show me over the boat. He was flogging a dead horse as far as I was concerned, then the electric steering failed, but as we didn't have such luxuries as this it didn't matter. The passengers and I all enjoyed the trip.

This was the year that our first daughter Jean was married, it only seemed a year or two since I was pushing her up to Telegraph in the pushchair, now she was twenty three and married. We were not losing her altogether as she married Bob, the under manager of the Co-Operative stores, just the other side of the road from us, which was very nice.

In 1976 I can see that we had twelve services starting in January and finishing on the 15th of December, one of these was to a catamaran the *Snow*

Goose, I remember it was a fair way to the South West of the Islands. A big Merchant ship had, I believe, just happened to crossed paths with her and those on the catamaran had managed to attract the skipper's attention. The weather made it impossible for the ship to help, other than to try to give them shelter and to call for us, and after a rough night we towed her back to St. Mary's.

Some of the services I can recall quite well, others are gone and at the moment forgotten until someone involved (of which sadly there are few left) or an old newspaper cutting comes to light. Many of these stories did not make the newspapers years ago, especially if anything happened on a weekend.

There was one other trip I remember quite well, it was not because of bad weather but because it was a flat calm with a long swell in the water. We were due for an exercise with a new inspector that evening but in the afternoon we had a call to meet a ship a few miles South West of the Bishop Light. She had an injured man onboard that needed hospital treatment, so we took Doctor Bell aboard also the new inspector who said that this would do as the exercise.

When we met the ship we found that she was a light ship (no cargo,) therefore floating very high in the water, her accommodation ladder was already lowered right aft and I could see that she was rolling far too much to use that, so we asked them to lower a pilot ladder instead. There was another snag, which was that because of her being so light in the water the round of her bottom in towards her propeller was too far away for us to reach with the boathooks to fender off while alongside the platform. After asking several times we realized that they could not speak or understand English, I then decided that I would try to get close enough to the platform of the companion ladder for the doctor to get aboard. He then could arrange with them to lower the man down the side of the ship when ready and also ask for a pilot ladder for his own evacuation.

As we approached the platform it was going right under water on the downward roll, then many feet in the air on the upward roll. The next minute there were two men coming down, one helping the other, and I then decided that it was just as well to try to get the injured man aboard because if we did not he could be washed overboard from the platform. We got the man aboard safely, then on the next upward roll the platform of the companion ladder knocked off the light on the top of our mast, then on the downward roll I had my hand out through the wheelhouse window trying to push it away but it now dismantled our starboard light on the top of the wheelhouse. I then went full ahead so that by the time she rolled down again we were clear. The inspector was in the wheelhouse during this time so I turned to him saying, 'That's a good start for your first visit here isn't it?' but he just said, 'Don't worry about it

Matt, I heard you ask for the other ladder several times and I reckon you did a good job getting him off like that without a lot more damage.' This chap turned out to be an ex-merchant navy officer with either a captain or mates ticket and therefore knew all about this sort of thing. The only thing he was wrong about was that I was not worried a damn about it anyway!

Another of the long dirty trips that was a 'no-service' was a May Day call from an Irish fishing boat *Dinosaur*, her position was somewhere about fifty miles North of the Islands and she was on passage from France I believe to Sligo in Ireland. She was completely disabled; the weather was bad with no ships in the area so off we went.

It was before radar and after going for some time we had a new position, which was quite a lot farther away which meant that we would not have enough fuel to risk towing her home and we would be much safer to tow her to Ireland when we found her. Our chart was on a big scale, one that did not give any detail of the Irish coast, but if we got to that hurdle I knew we could depend on the trawler skipper for any advice if it was needed. After steaming for about seven hours or so and on our reckoning we were now only about an hour or so away from him, a Naval frigate called us saying that he was close alongside and was taking him in tow to Ireland. So we now had another long trip home, but at least without the tow we had no fuel worries, this however was not the end of the story. During the next summer this boat turned up in our harbour one day with a keg or maybe two of Irish Guinness to say thank-you for trying to help and sorry for the trouble they had given us. I personally did not drink but many of the chaps did and Irish Bob became a great friend of mine and of many others of the fishing and boating community. Bob and his crew became a regular visitor in his boat every summer for a week or more, even when he changed his boat. He became very well known in Scilly, was well liked and with a great character, we still exchange Christmas cards even now.

There was one long trip that we were saved, but one, which at the time really annoyed me. The coastguard called one morning saying that a cargo ship was in trouble eighty miles West of the Bishop, he was listing badly needed immediate assistance and was in danger of sinking. The weather was really bad and there was a very big sea running. I at once asked if there were any ships near him because it would take us probably ten hours at least to reach him. The coastguard said that there were no other vessels around to help and the helicopters were not able to fly in this weather, so I said that as long as they knew we would be at least ten hours we would go.

We set off for an eighty-mile (at least) trip but before we had gone very far, we were told that the helicopter had now decided to try and we were to return, but to stand by alongside the pier. While we were listening in on the radio there was a message given out by Land's End Radio saying that, 'Due to the weather conditions the St. Mary's lifeboat had returned to station and two helicopters were now on their way.' This was a terrible insult to us and I should have made a complaint, but didn't. The helicopters did a marvellous job lifting off the crew and the ship did sink.

A good example of not making the newspaper headlines was the *Ra Rau*, which was a Romanian Stern Trawler factory ship, spy ship or whatever. This was at the time of the Cold War as it was called, the trawler had hit the Seven Stones rocks and was sure to be a total loss, but at the time we arrived another one of the same type was standing by. It was reasonable weather and the *Ra Rau's* crew had left her in their own lifeboats and boarded the standing by vessel. We went to her asking if all persons were safe, they assured us that they were but asked if we could return the Captain and two or three others to the *Ra Rau* and again return them to the vessel they were now on. We did this but one did not get much information out of those people in those times. After returning and putting them aboard the standing by ship and an assurance that we could not help any more we returned to St. Mary's. Both of these vessels bridge areas were like a forest of wireless aerials of all sorts, and in the morning the *Ra Rau* had taken her place among the many other fine looking vessels on the bottom around the Stones.

There was also a service to the sail training ship *Sir Winston Churchill*; this was a real lucky turn out for everyone. It started with my brother Harry, who lived in a cottage that looked out over the bay. He was looking out of his window; it was after dark, about eleven o'clock I think, when he saw some lights. He rang me saying that the lights were not flares but just like the flashing of a torch. Harry had served in the Royal Navy during the war and at one time trained as a signaller, but he told me that there was no definite signal of any sort, but he was worried, as it seemed to be low down on the water. I asked him to meet me, which he did in his car, but before leaving I asked Pat if she would phone the crew to ask them to go to the lifeboat house. I met Harry and we made our way by car to the pier, on the way Harry suggested that it may have been one of the Pilot gigs returning to St. Martins after a Gig race (and a drop of beer). This seemed very possible seeing that there had been no more flashing lights.

On reaching the pier we spent a short while watching in the direction Harry had pointed out and had decided that it must have been the gig. There were two men a little farther up the pier in the shelter of the higher back wall, also looking at times over the wall. We walked over to them and enquired if they had seen any lights. They had been there about fifteen minutes and had seen nothing, and said that they were from the *Sir Winston Churchill* (one was the

Mate) and were waiting for their tender, which had gone off to the ship a short while ago with some of their girl crew. On hearing this I turned to Harry saying, 'My God I bet that's what it was, get to the boathouse as quick as you can.' The two men asked if they could come with us and jumped into the back of the car.

When we arrived at the boathouse the doors were open and everything was ready, the crew on seeing us appear running, knew that there was something very wrong and all got aboard, and started the engines. Therefore, as soon as we were aboard there was the usual shout of, 'Let her go', the sound of the hammer on metal, and we were away. My brother and I had talked about the position already and we thought it was around the area of Carn Marvel so we set off at our best speed. I was trying to cut corners on the way and when about half way asked Bill to put the searchlight to shine on the next point of rocks because there was one off lying rock, which would be very low in or even under the water. I knew that if I could see the point I could then judge the distance and not waste too much time giving it a wide berth.

As Bill swung the searchlight beam around towards the point I saw a flash of yellow and shouted for him to turn it back, as it turned out I think that most of those aboard had probably seen it. This yellow was the eighteen to twenty foot tender sunk to her gunwales with eight girls and one man in charge all outside the boat hanging on. We went straight alongside, all of us helping to get them on to the lifeboat. They had been in the water hanging onto this sunken boat, which was rolling around in about a force six wind long enough, and were holding their hands up saying they could not hold on any longer. We got them all safely aboard and towing the tender was making for the pier, when the mate asked if I would put them aboard the *Winston Churchill*. On getting assurance that there was medical attention to be found there, also that he would be responsible, we put them aboard and returned to the slipway. I am certain that if Harry had not seen and reported these lights, some of them for sure would have drowned on what was by no means a bad night, but some were just about finished by the time we got them aboard.

The first call in 1979 is listed as, 'Sick man on trawler *Norse* of Hull, took out a Doctor'. I remember this one because, we had a new Doctor with us and it was his first trip on this sort of job, as far as I knew he had no experience of boating, and it was also a heavy gale. The trawler was down off the Bishop, the man was seriously ill and it was thought necessary to transfer him to the hospital. When we were quite close to the trawler I turned to the Doctor and explained how our crew would hold him with one foot on the rail, and when the time was right they would tell him to jump and he must get as high up the ladder as he could with his first jump. They would also help and lift him, but as soon as he got on the ladder he was to keep going up in case the boat came higher on the next wave. When coming back he was to stop when they told him and then jump for the deck when they shouted, and they would catch him to stop him from falling. There was quite a lot of rise and fall but he acted as if he had been doing this sort of thing all his life. The actual patient sadly had already died.

In 1980 we only did one service, this was to take off a sick seaman from an Irish vessel, this was also the last service of the *Guy and Clare Hunter* as our station boat, she had looked after us well and in all the dirty trips I had never ever been worried about the boat. Neither in all the years had we ever had any engine trouble of any kind in her, which was a great credit to all the different engineers over the years. Several of the crew were the same ones that had been aboard her on her very first service in 1956. The only changes in crew had been as when one man reached the retiring age of sixty (in those days), he was replaced by one of the young members of the slipway and emergency crew. By using this method there was always an experienced man on the slip, with young men to go to sea in the boat when necessary. Also, by keeping the same crew there was no trouble with anyone being first aboard in fine weather but not to be found in bad weather. It also meant that I could not be accused of favouritism, which I think goes a very long way towards keeping a good crew together. During all my time never did anyone leave the boat's crew with bad feeling. We all had, I believe, a special kind of friendship with those that are gone and those of us still here.

It was not all gales and big seas, sometimes the weather was calm and clear, and also we had a lot of fun. I remember one time we went out to investigate some flares or something of that nature, the report itself seemed a bit suspect but had to be checked out. There was just a fresh wind but it was very cold, the Honorary Secretary 'Trevelick' was at the boathouse and asked, 'Is it all right to come for a trip boy?' This was a matter of courtesy, so I of course replied, 'Yeah sure, get aboard,' knowing that he would be no trouble. He owned his own boat, had been born and lived in Scilly, also had served as mate on the Naval trawlers during the 1914 war.

We had been out searching for several hours when Trevelick who was in the cabin out of the spray and cold wind, pulled back the sliding door to the wheelhouse asking, 'What about a drop of soup boy?' (It was always boy!) 'Yes sure, help yourself, the key to the locker is hanging on the fire extinguisher,' I answered. 'Could you get it for us?' says Trevelick and so I get the soup while Roy takes over the wheel. Trevelick decides he will have tomato soup and so I put the tin on the floor of the cabin and got the knife to open it. These were self heating tins, one prised off a small cover which exposed a small wick, you then punctured the tin on both sides of the top of the can, between the wick and the edge of the can, then after lighting the fuse or wick, it only took about two minutes before it was really boiling hot. As I picked up the knife Trevelick says, 'It's all right boy I can do that,' so I returned to the wheelhouse taking over the wheel again. After about a minute I thought, 'I hope he remembered to puncture the can,' so I slid the door back saying, 'Did you remember ...' that was as far as I got – there was a hell of a bang, soup all over Trevelick, the deck head, sides of the cabin and everywhere else! He rubbed the soup from his face with his sleeve, picked up the can, the top of which had been blown off. I then say, 'Get another one, shall I?' 'No that's all right boy, there's still some left for me,' says he. We were all stiff with laughing but now had the job of washing the cabin down.

We went to take a sick man off from an Irish coaster one time, and as usual had a doctor with us, as we got close to him we asked him, 'Have you got a Pilot's ladder?' – this was for the Doctor to go aboard. He then replied, 'Yes sir, we have a Pilot ladder, but it is only a short one Sir.' This conversation was all going out over the radio, and Bill then replied, 'Will it reach the water Sir?' In his best Irish accent the man on the coaster says, 'I think it will.' 'O.K. then,' says Bill, 'Then we will use that one.' Again, we were curled up with laughter and some of the remarks from the comedians we had in the crew using their Irish accents did not improve matters a bit.

Another entertaining night we had, started with a call to give assistance to a Spanish trawler which had hit the Seven Stones and was making water fast. We had a relief boat on station at the time; she was a forty-five foot Watson with funnel and petrol engines. It was coming on dark and as we left the Islands I asked the 'travelling' mechanic to switch on the compass light, which he did but soon after when the boat fell with a bit of a bump, out went the light. This kept happening until the bulb was wedged with a sharpened match stick, we were now in good kilter, that is until when half way to the Stones there was a big bang and loads of sparks flying up in the air, as part of the engine silencer decided to part company with the funnel. So with the spirit of Dunkirk, Francis Drake and all the rest we carried on, sparks flying and the noise of a tank.

When we reached the Stones we found the trawler, now with a rope made fast to the stern of the Lightship. I went alongside to find some of her crew bailing water with buckets out of the fish room, by just reaching over to fill it and then empty it on the deck. I knew then that the vessel would go no deeper while her bulkhead was holding and so suggested we head for St. Mary's. The skipper was not having any of that, but I explained it was just as well to sink while trying to save her, as it was to sink tied up to the light vessel. In the end I got his confidence by saying that not only would we stay close to him but also I would put two of our crew aboard to help.

We then set off for home, I had put Roy and Harry aboard and told Roy to go about South West until he saw Peninnis Light and then turn straight in on the light, this would keep him clear of the Eastern Islands. He must have misheard or something because after about half an hour or so the trawler stopped. I immediately went to go alongside, telling Richard at the same time to swing the loud hailer around for me to speak. As he went to turn it, it just fell off; this was the end of our mishaps! On going alongside Roy wanted to know what I wanted him to do now as he had heard me say about seeing the Peninnis Light, but not the rest. We then carried on and when we were getting in towards the Eastern Islands the Steamship launch *Tean* with a fire pump, met us as arranged by wireless. This was put aboard and we arrived back with a poor young travelling mechanic, worried sick, but I knew that our problems had not been his fault. We had previous experience with that boat, and her normal mechanic (who was off sick), so I hoped I had helped to set his mind at rest.

There were many other trips searching for local boats that had not returned from a fishing trip on foggy evenings, these were a bit worrying sometimes, to be out among the rocks on a dark night with fog and just your own judgment. We never used a chart when around the islands, there was so much difference in directions and strength of the tide, altering all the time, and therefore it was far safer to trust to one's own knowledge.

There were little things one learnt, such as at night if one approached a big rock or island and the gulls were screaming or flying around, it usually meant that there was, or had been someone to disturb them, and so we would blow the fog horn and shout hoping for a reply. Sometimes if we thought we were in a certain place where there was shallow water with a ledge or sandy bottom we would shine the Aldis lamp down into the water to verify our position. On one of these occasions we were out all night around the Western rocks with no luck, but as daylight came in the boat was sighted by some of our shore crew, in an area that we had left a while before. The owner of the boat told me that we had passed very close to them on three occasions during the night, but without lights or anything he could not make his presence known.

On the 29th February 1980 I suffered a very bad accident while aboard the *J.M.L.* getting fitted up for the summer fishing season – it was nearly the end of everything for me. The boat was moored just off the old pier where many of them were kept in the shelter during the winter weather. There were luckily three other men working on their boats, Rodney who had been with me in the lifeboat crew for many years, Keith whose father had also been with us and Stuart who was to serve in the *Robert Edgar*. I was trying to adjust a dog clutch from the engine flywheel to my pot-hauling capstan when the spanner slipped. I then fell forward catching the collar of my overalls in a coupling of the capstan.

The engine driving the capstan was a ten-horse power Diesel and the capstan had a five to one reduction drive, this twisted me around the upright shaft at the same time tightening the clothes around my neck until the engine was brought to a stop. I of course knew nothing of this, it happened so fast and I was being strangled within seconds.

As luck would have it the Harbour Master was on the old pier, he had heard a thud and then my engine stopped. He then asked Rodney (whose boat was next to mine) to see if I was all right. Rodney then found me strung up around the capstan, Keith and Stuart then joined him and while two were cutting my clothes and getting me out of the foredeck the other was unmooring the boat which was moved to the pier. They had already told the Harbour Master to phone for the ambulance and a Doctor, by the time they reached the pier Doctor Wooltorton was there waiting. A phone call then was made to hold the local helicopter, which was ready for take off, and to make room for a stretcher case. We stopped at the hospital for more drugs (the Doctor already having given me some injections) then carried on to the helicopter and straight to Penzance Hospital. One of the helicopter pilots that helped save my life that day was one of those picked up by us at the time of the helicopter accident, which I will tell of later. Coincidently he was the one, which I myself had grabbed by the back of his shirt to keep him up in the water and then helped to lift aboard.

All this I have been told since, I was unconscious from the first second or two and was so badly strangled that the blood was coming out of my ears and nose, having burst the blood vessels in my head. My head and face were so swollen and discoloured that the airport and ambulance men lifting me aboard did not even know who I was, some of them had known me all their lives. I was in Penzance hospital within about seventy-five minutes, which was a great credit to everyone and I obviously owe my life to those involved all along the line, from the Harbour Master, boatmen and helicopter staff to the hospital, Doctors and medics at Penzance. My family and myself will always be grateful. The Doctor had told me afterwards that they had been doubtful if I would make it.

The next morning I opened my eyes at about four o'clock in the morning, Doctor Wooltorton who had come with me was on my right, he just said, 'Hello Matt,' and I replied, 'Hello Doc!' – the expression on his face of disbelief, I will never forget. He then said, 'Do you know me?' I thought, 'What a stupid question,' and replied, 'Of course I bloody do, you're Doctor Wooltorton aren't you?' He was amazed, so just looked across and says, 'Doctor Bell is there,' and I looked across at him saying, 'Hello Doc,' and then passed out again.

To cut a long story short Penzance hospital took pictures for their records saying that they had never seen anyone recover from such a state, my face and head were very swollen and all colours, the whites of my eyes were now all purple – this of course I first saw when I was given a mirror. It took about six weeks I think for my eyes to clear, but when this happened my dark brown eyes were and still are a sort of mixed dark blue. After a day or two I was transferred to our own hospital. Pat, Jean and Lucy had not been allowed to see, or come with me to Penzance hospital and had flown over the next morning and so we returned together a day or two later.

When in the hospital I heard the Doctors talking quietly about my injured arm and one of them says that the specialist had said I would never use my arm again. The new lifeboat was due before very long so I thought, 'I bloody well will.' They told me not to try, but at night I would lift my useless arm up with my good one and grab hold of the grip above my bed, I then would pull and swing about on it. After I was home again I used to lift the useless arm up to the top of a door and then swing on it. One day I got aboard the punt and by using one arm and trapping the oar under my knees I got under way and could row. After that I made great strides and within six weeks I was now passed as fit to go back in the lifeboat and my fishing boat again. The specialist would not believe that I could use that arm until many months after Doctor Bell saw me using it as normal.

German lifeboat and 'Guy and Clare Hunter'.

CHAPTER 7

FAMOUS TRIPS

IN 1967 WE had a wreck that made headlines both here and in many places around the world. This was the biggest Tanker in the world, the *Torrey Canyon*, being 118,285 tons, her length 974 feet and a beam of 125 feet – nearly as wide as a football pitch and as long as three end to end. She was only 57 feet shorter than the *Queen Elizabeth* and she hit the Seven Stones at a speed of 17 knots on the fine clear morning of March 18th. We launched at 9.20 am, and on sighting her she really seemed massive. As soon as we arrived we went alongside and asked the Captain what he needed us to do. We were asked to stand by in case of evacuation as he had tugs on their way to try and get her off, but knowing that she had hit the rocks doing 17 knots and was a loaded ship, we did not give much chance of her getting off again. When we were about two or three miles from her we ran into the oil, one minute the boat was a showpiece of brilliant paint and shining brass work and then we dived into the next wave putting the bow under water, when right down the deck came what looked like a slimy brown jelly about two or three inches thick. It went over everything in its path, the deck, the paint and brass work and everywhere as it made it's way aft and over the side. It was like this all the time afterwards, but we found owing to the sea state being big enough for us to be taking water over the bow, also throwing quite a lot of spray over the rest of the boat, the oil did not stick but just slithered over the side again. Although everything was slimy and slippery, at least the worst of it was going back over the side. On reaching the wreck we realised that she was on the Pollard rock, just under her bridge, and that gave us a good idea where the other rocks were – Flat Ledge astern and then the Flemmie and South Rock, with the North East Ledge on the Starboard bow and abeam and running down to the South East Rock. We now knew that there was plenty of water alongside, except for under her bridge. While we were steaming around her to have a good look, a helicopter (I believe it was a Wessex) arrived. After flying around for a while he spoke to us on the radio, saying that they hadn't had time for breakfast, so we sent up our tin of biscuits and some chocolate, which was our rations for long trips.

Things started moving fast, the Trinity House Vessel *Stella* arrived and took up a position about three quarters of a mile ahead of her. A tug the *Utrecht* then also arrived and stopped about a quarter of a mile away. She then called us on the radio asking us if we could transfer two of their men, one a wireless operator and the other a deck officer – I think this was to set up a salvage

Torrey Canyon.

contract with the *Torrey Canyon*. The *Utrecht* was lying across the sea, probably to give us a lee. I went in on an angle at the forward end of her working deck and there were the two men waiting to board. It was quite easy to jump onto our side, catching the rail and getting aboard. One did this, but the other didn't. The *Utrecht* was rolling and heaving to leeward on each roll and to save contact I went astern quickly, but then judging that I still had enough angle and time I went ahead again to allow the other man to board. As soon as he boarded I went full astern but the tug had moved side on down the sea, she then rolled the other way and by this time we were abreast and under her counter stern. I could see the stern dropping right onto our bow, but as it fell it passed in front of our stem head with just inches to spare, a big splash sending the water everywhere. We had no trouble putting the men onto the tanker, as she was a dead ship.

Early after mid-day the coastguard asked for a situation report and I suggested that in my opinion, for what it was worth, there was not much chance of getting her off, but that she would probably break her back and they may then tow off the stern half. Other vessels were now arriving, Royal Navy vessels and a trawler with newsmen, also there were more tugs on the way.

In the late afternoon through hearing some radio chat, the *Utrecht* heard that because of giving our tin of biscuits to the helicopter chaps we now had had nothing to eat since our breakfast. She then called us telling us to come alongside in about half an hour, when they sent across soup, bread, butter and some lovely hot rissoles, and some tinned fruit all of which were very welcome.

When it came dark we took up a position on her Port side steaming slowly up and down. In the early hours we heard a big tearing, crashing noise and all the lights went out. I knew then that she must have broken her back and could drop off the rock into deep water, so went full ahead and onto her Starboard side ready to take them off if necessary. By then the emergency lighting was on and there did not seem to be any panic, but we could see that she had now started to list to Starboard. The *Utrecht* had made an attempt to tow her off in the evening, but there was no chance. By the next morning she had increased her list and had gone down by the head with the water washing in over her Starboard bow. The *Torrey Canyon* called us by radio, asking us to take off fourteen of his crew. Because we considered it would be better for everyone if we could put them on the *Stella*, we called him up and he was very pleased to help and so this was done.

The weather forecast was now very important but disappointing. The forecast was that the wind would now freshen from the North West to the North East, up to gale force and the Captain then asked for another eighteen men to be taken off. Because of the now strong and still freshening wind, we went alongside and placed the boat in a position so that as we rose up on the waves we were just about level with her deck. The men could easily jump aboard, where our crew would help steady them. As there was quite a good rise and fall of twelve to fifteen feet I considered this a safer option than using a ladder.

If a ladder was used there was a very good chance of one of them being squashed or having his legs broken between the boats. We had taken off eight of the crew with no trouble, but the ninth man did not jump when he was told. He then changed his mind and he fell between the ship and us. Luckily I had told the bowman that we would use just one rope and that he was not to make fast, but just to take a couple of turns around the bollard and hold on to it. As soon as I saw from the wheelhouse that the man had missed, I came full astern shouting to Richard the bowman to let go. The lifeboat was thrown against the ship with a crash, smashing the nine inch belting into pieces – my heart was in my mouth thinking the man had most certainly been very badly hurt, if not killed. As soon as we bounced off George and Rodney were shouting that he was all right and we had come astern far enough to give him the shelter of our shoulder. We now got him around the bow and aboard but the rest of the men refused to come and so two helicopters came and took them off.

I was worried about the condition of the man and so contacted Doctor Bell by radio. I explained what had happened and after some questions about him

Doctor Bell says, 'Don't worry Matt he will be all right, I will arrange for Penlee to relieve you.' When the Penlee lifeboat arrived we met her and as all the rocks were now under water we led her down through the rocks. When this nice shiny boat hit the oil we could hear the groan and I'm sure they reckoned we did it on purpose.

I believe we arrived home at about half past six in the evening. We set off to relieve the Penlee boat again at five o'clock the next evening and stood by for the night returning on the morning of the 21st. I had just got indoors when again we were called, there had been an explosion, one man seriously injured needed a Doctor and so within ten minutes we were on our way. One of the smaller tugs was heading for Newlyn with the man aboard and so we now returned having been at sea for a total of fifty-four hours, thirty-three of them on one stretch.

I was later asked to attend a meeting in the Town Hall about the spraying of oil, also attending were Government men, Naval officers, the Chairman of the Council and also the Steamship Company Chairman. The Steamship Company were very keen to get on with spraying, but I objected saying that unless we had a wind from the South East we would not get the oil. This was unbelievable as we were closest to the wreck, but I was afraid of the damage the detergent would do. So, I really stuck my neck out, warning that if spraying started in the Islands I would report that it was not necessary. I was then asked how did I know that the oil would not come ashore on the Islands? To which I replied that I had seen at least four wrecks on the Stones and nothing came to Scilly without a South East wind.

We never had any spraying; neither did we have any oil. As expected it came within three quarters of a mile and then went on past the Eastern Isles, right down to France. Later the ship broke again, this time aft of the bridge and she was then set on fire after several attempts by bombing aircraft.

We suffered from the *Torrey Canyon* for a long time afterwards. Around this time we used to do quite a bit of Mullet fishing but after the wreck we did not get any catches for many years.

About two months after the *Torrey Canyon* we were called out to assist the Motor yacht *Braemar*, from which Land's End Radio had received a May Day call, giving her position as twenty-eight miles South South West of Bishop Rock. She was a steel yacht of nearly two hundred tons, length was one hundred and twenty five feet, beam eighteen feet four inches, and was under contract to I.T.N. to get the first T.V. pictures of Sir Francis Chichester's return from his single handed around the world voyage. The May Day message stated

Beginning to tow the 'Braemar'.

that she was taking in water in the engine room, one of her two engines was stopped, the other was not likely to be long before it also stopped, she was heading towards Falmouth at five knots and required immediate assistance. We launched at about 6.45 am, and on clearing St. Agnes set a course to intercept her. This was not easy as it was a force nine South West wind at that time and I knew that although they had reported a speed of five knots this had to be wrong and so allowed for her being much faster. Shortly after 9.00 am she reported that both engines were now stopped and she was drifting with the wind and current.

We had now passed the point of interception and were going towards the Lizard at full speed. We had contact with a merchant vessel the *Trader*, which was in the vicinity also searching for her but could not find her, until the Captain had a brilliant idea. This was to get the skipper of the *Braemar* to let him know every time the *Braemar* was in a rainsquall; he then plotted them from his radar and headed in her direction. As soon as he found her he passed on the position to us, it worked out to be about two and a half miles ahead of us as we had been going, and in about twenty minutes we had found them. The *Trader* was attempting to get a line aboard by rocket and after a couple of attempts agreed to let us pass a line for him. We picked up the line and passed it to some men on the bow, as we passed we were that close and on the top of a wave that it was just handed over. We now stood by while they connected a tow line, this was done by all of them lining up and pulling it by hand, all power having been lost with the engine failure.

We watched the *Trader* gradually pull but the *Braemar* was a little side on and she started listing to Port as the pull increased. We thought that she was going right over but the mooring bits were torn right out of her deck taking the bow rails etc. with them, and the *Braemar* now righted herself again. The *Trader* wanted us to pass the tow again but the *Braemar* skipper said that there was nothing to make it fast to, also they did not think that they would be able to get it aboard again. The *Trader* now said that as he could be of no more assistance and the lifeboat was standing by he would proceed on his voyage.

While we were wondering what was to happen I noticed a big coil of rope on the *Braemar's* forward deck and on asking, was told by him that it was nylon. We then said that if he gave us the end of it we would try to get him into Newlyn, the tow was passed and we started off at a snail's pace. The *Braemar* kept heading to the Northward because unknown to us the rudder was jammed, and so five times we parted the rope. It was then made fast the anchor chain but at one time we only made good a half a mile in two hours of towing. The wind and sea had both increased, darkness was coming in and so I told them that I thought it was time to take them off and we would still try to get her into Newlyn. The skipper agreed, but stated that the engineer, one other and himself would like to stay aboard. I agreed as long as they would abandon her in the rubber dinghy, which was ready if I told them to. We then cast off the tow and went alongside on the Starboard side. She was rolling badly, but as she rolled they were able to jump from the top rail with our men ready to grab their arms. We took off fifteen men and one woman, two men had held her sitting on the rail and pushed her off into the arms of our crew members, we had very little room and there were some nasty obstructions but all went well and we took up the tow again.

The skipper had previously said that he expected her to sink within twelve hours after her second engine stopped – this time was well passed. At ten o' clock that night it was now blowing force ten right onto the shore to which the *Braemar* was trying to head, there was also heavy thunder and lightning. I asked Roy to take the wheel while I again checked the radar, while I was doing so Roy shouts through the cabin door to tell me that we were very close to the cliffs as those on deck could now see the waves breaking on the rocks. I had noticed on the radar that we were now only a quarter of a mile off the shore. I told him that it was O.K.; I again took over the steering deciding to have one more try at turning the *Braemar* away from the shore. Luckily I caught her on the top of a wave and now headed out for the Lizard Light to give us some sea room. We eventually got her into Newlyn harbour at twenty-five minutes past two in the morning.

During the tow the *Scillonian* was on her way to Penzance, we did not see her but Captain Thomas had asked if they could help but I had told him that I didn't think it was possible. He then told me that a tug had been engaged again on a Lloyds salvage claim, but after steaming one hour West of the Lizard had returned to Falmouth. He also told me that he had shipped the biggest sea over his stern that he had ever done since being her Captain, which was for a number of years.

When we arrived in Newlyn I was asked if there was a Doctor available, but after calling and searching for one, I returned to the boat to find that the man who had been very badly seasick had been taken ashore by his mates – most of which had also been badly seasick.

We set off again for Scilly after a meal, the first of anything to eat since the night before. It was now about 4.00 am, still blowing just as bad but we were very pleased to be able to proceed at our normal speed with no worries, and we arrived in Scilly at about 8.30 that morning. We had been on service for twenty-seven hours, thirteen hours of which was towing the *Braemar* a distance of sixteen miles. In some reports and articles I have read the speed at which we were towing has been badly over estimated. For instance it has been stated that at one time we were only making a speed of four knots instead of what was in fact a quarter of a knot. Another stated that we were at one time making as little as three knots – I would have been a lot happier at the time if these things had been true.

The man that was so ill and who was taken to hospital by his friends sadly died two days later. We had a very nice letter from his mother asking us not in any way to blame ourselves for his death, as it was found that he was suffering from heart troubles unknown to him or his parents and unsuspected by the hospital. She also thanked us for what we had done for him and she wanted us to know that she was sorry for the way some of the newspapers etc. were criticising us, for not leaving the ship and bringing him ashore. I know that some of those at R.N.L.I. Head Office were also doing that at the time, but I hope that they felt ashamed of themselves when the truth was known.

Many years after, an ex-wartime spitfire pilot Wing Commander Potter had bought the *Braemar* and he brought her to Scilly for us to renew our acquaintance with her. I had the pleasure of taking her around the rocks and Islands for a day or two each summer for a couple of years, while Pat, Marie and Mr. Potter sunned themselves on the afterdeck. The crew on that rescue was myself, Roy Guy, Bill Burrow, Richard and Harry Lethbridge, Fred

Woodcock, Rodney Terry and George Symons. The crew were all presented with vellums, Roy and Bill with Bronze medals and myself with a Silver medal.

I also received many compliments after the *Braemar* service from men who had served with, and who were old enough to be my Father, telling me that if ever I was short of crew they would be quite willing to go with me. These people and the compliments they gave were very special to me. Above all, as I walked up the slipway, Dad came to meet me, patted me on the shoulder and said, 'That was a good job you did there boy'. This was the first time in my life he had ever been able to show his feelings and I know how much it had meant to him.

Before I leave this part of the story about twenty-five to thirty years later a gentleman and his wife came to see me one evening at home. He stood on the doorstep with his hand held out to shake mine. I had asked him inside but he said; 'Now before I come in I will tell you something. I was a Captain of the Harrison Line on passage on the *Trader* when you were out to the *Braemar*, and I was asked to keep the deck log at that time.' I read the deck log afterwards, in which it stated that while the *Trader* was stopped she was taking water over all. He then told me that as they were leaving he turned to the Captain of the ship and told him, 'One day I am going to visit those Islands and shake that man's hand'. As people will realise these things are also a compliment to the crew, and coming from other seamen that understand, they are very special.

1970 started with poor weather and on the 21st of February, at around two o'clock in the morning we were called out to the aid of a Swedish ship the *Nordanhav*. She was of four hundred and fifty ton and her cargo (grain I believe) had shifted, giving her a very serious list to Port. She was about thirty-five miles North North East of Round Island and it was blowing a gale, with squalls of rain and of course it was dark. We launched and went up through the channel between Tresco and Bryher, and then set off on what we knew was going to be a long old trip.

While we were heading towards her we were also listening to the wireless traffic between her and any other vessels, also Land's End Radio. There were two merchant vessels and a Frigate the *H.M.S. Ulster* in the area, which were heading for her at their best speed. After the *H.M.S. Ulster* reached her we had a message passed from the Honorary Secretary at St. Mary's (Doctor Bell) to St Mary's Lifeboat, 'At the coxswain's discretion you may return to station,' to which I replied that we would continue until the crew was safe. I thought to myself, 'Yes Doc, you knew dammed well what the answer would be before you sent it.' This was much to the disappointment of some who thought we would just take a beating for nothing, and that the Frigate would take them all off. I said that they would be very lucky to be able to take the crew off on a night like it was, and so we would continue until they had.

We heard messages being passed that the *Ulster* were trying their best to take off the crew by drifting life rafts down to them on lines etc., but as the night wore on they were having no luck. When we had been steaming for about three hours a search aircraft circled us, then tried to lead us off to Starboard but I guessed that he had most likely seen an empty life raft and so continued on our course.

Due to the state of the weather our radar was of no use to us and so we had to depend on our own dead reckoning. When we were about four hours on the way and in my reckoning about one hour from the *Nordanhav* (whose wireless was now silent), we called the *Ulster* for a long count so that we could take a bearing if possible. After taking a bearing, which was within ten degrees either side of our bow (very good taking into account the way we were being thrown around), I then asked the *Ulster* if she would take one of us. As this was a more stable ship and should be a good check, we then gave her a long count and soon after she called us up giving me their bearing of us. This did not agree with mine in any way and so now I had a problem. I was very sure of my own reckoning but how do I ask a warship if she is wrong? I then asked her if she meant we were North or South of her and she replied by asking me what I considered my position to be. I was all prepared for this and so passed our position in latitude and longitude, plus any bearing and distance from her. She asked us to wait; I expect she had been checking while we had been talking, I had also told her that we had been four hours on dead reckoning. After a short time she called again telling us, 'You are dead right old man, ours is a class C bearing,' this was a great boost, but I wondered what was happening on the bridge and who was getting a dressing down! About an hour after we could see the lights of the *Ulster* not far ahead of us but no lights of the *Nordanhav*, on asking for her position the *Ulster* put their search light on her and kept it there. When I first saw her she was rolling her side under and could have turned over at any time. I told the boys to get all our fenders out on the Starboard side.

She was only about a quarter of a mile away but as it was still dark and all her power had failed, until the *Ulster* switched his search light on we could not see her at all. We were still going at full speed and I could now see the crew standing on the hatch in front of the bridge, which was aft. As we got closer I could see that this was the only place for us to try to get them off, but we were hampered for space by a rope ladder and a half sunk rubber dinghy. We went straight in close alongside and beckoned the men to jump and we would catch them. At first they were not at all keen, then one left the safety of the hatch, ran to the rail and jumped as the ship rolled towards us. He landed perfectly safely and was taken to the cabin. When she rolled towards us her rails went right under water but on the way the ship gave us a crash sending us far enough away that when her side came up she was clear of us. We had Rodney, Richard and Harry forward catching the crew, Bill looking after the engines and radio, Les and myself aft and Roy Guy showing them to the cabin. After getting the boat into position I would let go the wheel and help to catch anyone aft, while they were catching one forward as she rolled up at the same time. Sometimes one jumped and sometimes two, one forward and one aft, each time there were some awful crashes etc. and we had to hold the lifeboat side on until the *Nordanhav* rolled down to us. Again after ten men were aboard without injury, which was unbelievable, I was faced with the problem of getting away from her. I could not go astern because of the raft and it's rope, also the ships ladder but if I just went ahead the ship would heave down on us before we cleared. The next time she gave us a clout and knocked us sideways about twenty feet, I went full ahead going along her side towards the bow. I could not turn too much or the quarter would touch the side of the *Nordanhav* and then I would lose control. As we approached the bow she was again rolling toward us and as we passed out under the curve of her bow I was watching the anchor pass just over the top of our wheelhouse still rolling down and then watching it just miss our rails as we passed under it at full speed.

As soon as we were clear I turned the boat into the wind and went out to lean over to see how badly we were damaged. I was thinking that if it was very bad I could put the rescued crew aboard the *Ulster* with some of our crew, keeping one engineer and one other to return to St. Mary's asking the *Ulster* to escort us back. This was not necessary but they did call us asking what we were going to do with the crew of the *Nordanhav* and would we like to put them aboard. I thought about it but as we had taken them off without injury it would have been stupid to risk trying to get them aboard her, the way she was rolling about. So I thanked him but refused the offer and turned for home. We were having a nasty old trip on the way, as the weather was still the same and at one time I handed over the wheel to the 2nd coxswain so that I could check something on the chart in the cabin. While I was there one of the men says, 'The Captain wants to know – if this boat roll over, she come up again?' This made me smile as I told him, 'No if this boat go over, she stay over!' I suppose they were not used to all the crashing around that we were doing, much different to a large ship. I believe it was at this same time that one of the men who was at first sitting on one of the seats just in front and below me, under the shelter of the wheelhouse feeling quite ill (seasick) got off the seat and sat on the deck inside the wheelhouse leaning back onto the engine room bulkhead. The water from the scuppers was sloshing back and forth, sometimes three or four inches deep, but as cold and miserable as he was he would not move into the cabin or anything but stayed like that all the way home, another five hours or more.

Again I got a little pat on the shoulder and a, 'Well done boy,' from Dad. Roy and Bill were both again given a Bronze medal and myself Silver, the crew all again receiving the 'Thanks on Vellum' for this service. I did not go up to get the medal this time and so Doctor Bell picked it up on my behalf.

1977 was a bad year for me, one that I will always remember; we were called out to look for a French fishing boat *The Enfant de Bretagne* at five past two in the morning of February 13th. The message was received by Falmouth coastguard, which had now taken over for search and rescue from Land's End Radio. It was thought that there was a French fishing vessel aground on rocks near the Bishop Rock Lighthouse, this message had been very garbled and no other contact could be made with the boat. We launched at 02.15, with a strong South Westerly wind and a very heavy ground sea as we call it, there was no moon therefore quite a dark night.

My first intentions were to go straight down Broad Sound to the Bishop watching for lights or any other indication as to exactly which rocks the fishing boat was on, as the message which had been received covered a very big area. When we were about half-way and just before getting to Annet, we heard Falmouth coastguard asking the Bishop if they had seen any lights or flares anywhere. They replied that the only thing that they had seen about an hour before was a ship's lights coming up from the South East. On hearing this I knew from my own experience that at night it is very hard to tell how far away a light is also whether it is a small vessel not far away or a larger one a long way away. The other thing that made me decide to alter course was that knowing the area quite well I knew that the bearing would be in a line with the Gilstone Ledges and Pednathise Head.

So I changed my course going South down Smiths Sound so that I could cover all the rocks on the South East side, from the entrance of Smiths Sound right along to the Gilstones without any waste of time, also with a very good chance of finding the trawler on the Gilstone Ledges. As soon as we cleared Smith Sound those of the crew on the foredeck shouted that they could smell diesel oil. I was now sure that we were on the right track, because of the direction of the wind and tide, so we carried on at full speed until we came to Melledgan Island. We then fired a parachute flare to make sure there was nothing in that area. I did not expect to find anything because we were now passing through quite a lot of small bits of polystyrene, which meant that the main wreckage must still be ahead of us.

The next rocks were Gorregan Island, we sent off some more parachute flares, one on the East and one on the West side and then carried on until we were South of the next likely place. These flares showed up an area of continuous rocks from Pednathise Head right up along as far as the light would reach. This was now out to the South West end of the rocks of Scilly with nothing to break the heavy South West ground sea. The water around these rocks was just a mass of swirling white water and spray shooting up into the air.

As the flare came down we thought we saw something that to us was the bow of a French trawler and a part of her mast showing. I immediately thought that she was on some rocks at the back of the ones in front of us and so we went around Pednathise Head cutting between the Old Bess Ledges and Pednathise, which is a very narrow passage. At the time I thought that I had misjudged it, but we were all right and now out the back of the rocks. We fired a couple more flares but could not find anything, I then decided to try to locate it again from inside and so passed the Old Bess again and around Pednathise Head. We stopped at the entrance of a gap between some of the rocks, which locally we call the Neck of the Daisy.

On firing another flare and with the searchlight we now saw again the bow of the wooden trawler and part of her mast showing, as we were going towards it at times the corner of the wheelhouse showed between the swells. This neck between the rocks is very narrow and can only be used by those who know it in fine weather at the right state of tide. In places it was not much wider than our boat's length, also there is no room to turn around when in the neck, and so this would mean a dog's leg turn out through, if we entered it. As we were going in slowly, trying to see through all the spray etc. we saw two men lying on their stomachs holding onto the bow railings. We were now very nearly into the neck, when a very heavy sea came in over Pednathise Head burying it down with a roar of noise and at the same time I knew that we had to get out to try another way.

The flare had now gone out, the searchlight for some reason also went out, all in a split second and I knew from having fished that area for many years that the only chance was to go full ahead and hard to Port. As soon as she started turning to Port I knew that I had to turn hard to Starboard, hoping to get out through the neck and at the same time hoping that we would not hit some shallow rocks on the outer end. This I did without seeing anything on the way, after getting outside the Aldis light and then the searchlight came back on and I heard one on deck say, 'God, did we come through that neck then?' The reply was, 'We bloody well must have, as we are outside now', so the crew had not seen anything but breaking water either.

As soon as we were outside I once more came close around Pednathise Head again, having also asked the crew to get the anchor ready, with the idea of dropping it outside the neck then passing the rope out over our stern on the way in to the trawler. I knew that we would most likely be severely damaged and have our propellers fouled, but if the men could jump to us, we then perhaps could pull ourselves outside with the capstan and anchor rope, then if need be we could call for someone to come and tow us home.

The time taken to get through the neck and back to the entrance was only about three minutes, as soon as we got there we fired off another flare and by the light of the flare and searchlight all we could see was part of the bow and foredeck on top of a rock about twenty feet high. There was a mass of boiling water with part of a rubber dinghy which was still fastened to something under water, plus a lot of pieces of wood and wreckage from the size of a matchbox to the size of part of a wheelhouse, pieces of decking and allsorts, but of the men there was no sign.

We had already radioed for a helicopter in case there was anyone up on top of the rocks with the big part of her bow. We had gone into the entrance again but could not see the top of the rock because of its height. While waiting we kept looking with the searchlight without much hope, knowing that the men we saw must have been smashed amongst the rocks because of the wave direction etc.

When the helicopter came we again went into the entrance of the neck shining our searchlight on to the top of the rocks. At first they said the spray was going to high for them to see, but eventually they were able to see that there was no one there. After this we searched farther afield, the helicopter picked up one body and later saw another that was too close in for them to reach, so we recovered the second body which we later passed up to them. Neither of them were damaged by rocks and must have been washed over before the trawler got in the rocks, because the next day or so I found where she had hit another rock on the way in.

After searching well into the day we returned to St. Mary's. I cannot describe our feelings. The main thing was of course, sorrow for those that had been lost. But then there was almost disbelief that after we had been so close to them we still had been unable to save them. They had been hanging on for about an hour hoping that someone would come, and after seeing us coming in towards them, not more than forty feet away they must have felt sure that they were now safe. They probably did not see anything until the wave hit them. It was against all odds that we should have found them as soon as we did, that they had not been washed away sooner, and that this particularly big sea, had been strong enough to tear apart such a big piece of the vessel, and to have thrown it up to that height on the rocks.

I felt awfully cheated because we had not been able to get them, it was also the first time in twenty years that we had not been able to do what we had wanted to, through no fault of our own. In fact we all knew that we ourselves had been unbelievably lucky to get away with it as we did.

After we had re-housed the boat we made everything ready for another call out, the crew were as usual just saying, 'Is that the lot?' and, 'Is it O.K. to go?' to which I usually said, 'Yes O.K. fine,' but as one of them went out of the door he said, 'Well thanks for the trip, and thanks for bringing us back.' It probably took a lot of nerve for any of these men to say a thing like that, but it did show how lucky he thought we had been.

The crew on this service were Roy Guy, Bill Burrow, Rodney Terry, George Symons, Harry Lethbridge, Roy Duncan and myself. The crew were again awarded Vellums and myself a Silver medal.

One thing I shall never forget was the following afternoon, I had walked up to see a very good and old friend of mine, Norman Jenkins, the friendship was and is from Grandfathers to Grandsons. As I walked in the sitting room door he was in his usual chair, he just looked me straight in the eye and he said, 'You can't win them all you know boy.' That was all that was necessary, he knew exactly how I was feeling he had been through it himself in past years. Brian his son told me that his Dad had told him that he had only one regret in his lifetime. Not understanding Brian asked, 'What regrets can you have?' he then replied, 'I regret that I had not been young enough to go to sea in the lifeboat with Boy Matt.' Again this was something very special in my book.

There was something else that came back to my mind after this service. I believe it was a couple of years earlier, when we were in this area with the German lifeboat, the then director of the R.N.L.I. was with us, and when I went in fairly close to some rocks to show them the seals on the rocks, one of the ladies aboard remarked how good it was to be in so close to them. This director sarcastically replied something like, 'Yes, if you are trying to impress people, but normally it's not the sort of thing one does.' At the time I thought, 'If I wanted to impress anyone mate, I would have gone through the neck.' This was in daylight, but not so long after we were there in a big sea and the middle of the night. I wished he had been with us, to see how wrong and stupid his clever remarks were!

August 14th 1979 was another special day, we were called out to go the aid of a yacht called the *Magic*; she was one of the three hundred and three yachts that were taking part in the Fastnet Yacht Race. It was about 3 o'clock in the morning, there was a very deep depression over the area and the winds at this time were gusting to force twelve from West North West. We set off at full speed as usual; it was going to be a dirty long old trip. The yacht was forty-two or three miles to the North West of the Islands and so it meant a punch, head on to the sea all the way.

R.N.L.B. 'Guy and Clare Hunter' searching for Fastnet Race yachts.
© Crown copyright 1979/MOD. Reproduced with the permission of the Controller of Her Majesty's Stationery Office.

When we were about half way towards the position we passed a big racing yacht running down towards the Bishop, she was under storm rig but going like a train, it was a sight worth seeing on such a night but it only lasted less than a minute before she was gone again. By the wireless signals this yacht seemed to be Ted Heath's *Morning Cloud*.

Soon afterwards we heard a message from the Fishery Protection vessel *H.M.S. Alderney* that she was also making for the *Magic*, so we took a bearing of her signal, and on taking another each time she transmitted, I could tell that we would both arrive at the same time. As we were already going at our full speed, there was nothing we could do about that. We met as expected but there was no *Magic*, this was also to be expected and so we started a search.

By this time the May Day signals were coming through thick and fast from a number of yachts. We next sighted one that was dismasted with a drogue rope out over the stern but a helicopter was also in sight; they informed us that they had taken off those aboard just as we got to them. In company with *H.M.S. Alderney* we then headed for another position farther to the North, where there was another yacht in trouble. After some time, I believe it was about 10 am; we came across another yacht the *Victride*. She was having a hard time of it running before the seas with a very small storm jib but seemed to be all right, so we carried on with the *Alderney* again to look for one, which had been reported twelve miles farther North of us. Sometime later we received another call for assistance from the *Victride*, so the *Alderney* continued North to search and we turned back to find the *Victride*. By our reckoning we were now about sixty miles or more North West of Scilly, while steaming North with the *Alderney* she was a lovely sight charging into the seas which seemed to be going right into her bridge, while we were going up one side and down the other but right through the tops of the waves many times.

We soon found the *Victride* again, with the help of another helicopter, which had arrived, and they reported that they had been knocked down and their cabin hatch was split so they were taking in water. At this stage they did not want to leave her but wanted an escort to St. Mary's. We now turned back for St. Mary's keeping close to her, on two occasions she broached but righted herself then with the help of the wind in her storm jib got back on course again. After we started for home there was another call from a yacht called the *Pegasus*, also requesting an escort, so we then arranged an interception course for each of us and we met her at about 6.00 pm North of the Islands. We were heading to pass to the East side of the Islands and then in the Crow Sound passage, all went well and we arrived back at St. Mary's at about 8.00 pm. The shore crew was refuelling the lifeboat while we got a change of dry clothes, but while this was happening another yacht was asking for assistance a few miles North West of Round Island. She had a rudder failure and so half an hour after arriving we were off again, the weather had now eased quite a lot but was still not very nice. We met the *Festina Tertia* about nine or ten miles West of Round Island, she had I believe lost a man overboard earlier. We towed her back to St. Mary's via Tresco Channel getting home at about 11.30 pm, nearly twenty one hours since starting out.

The weather moderated away during the night and the next morning the local boats were out fishing or looking for their gear. I found that I had lost eighty-five out of one hundred pots.

The new fast Falmouth lifeboat which had set out to look for any stray yachts the night following the troubles, before this she had been helping a cruising yacht off Falmouth I believe, searched but could not find any more. A Naval vessel that had been towing one arranged to meet her off the Bishop where she passed her tow over to the Falmouth boat to take into St. Mary's.

There were framed certificates given to the crews of all lifeboats including Falmouth that took part in the Fastnet service.

Our first really bad weather trip in an Arran Class lifeboat the *Robert Edgar* was a very sad one. The Penlee lifeboat was called out to a coaster, the *Union Star*, late in the afternoon of 19th December 1981. At about midnight the telephone rang, it was a call from Les Vipond, our District Inspector, saying that the *Solomon Browne* had not returned yet and he was asking if we would be willing to come over to Land's End to look for her if necessary. I replied that we would come right away, but was told to wait while they were checking some information. It was a very nasty night, which has been recorded in many books and newspapers, and therefore I will only write of what happened as near as I can, in our case.

As soon as Les finished his call I phoned all the crew and called Rodney from next door telling them that it looked as if something had happened to the Penlee boat and I wanted them all to come to our house, ready to go. It seemed impossible to grasp that anything could have happened, but in our hearts we knew ourselves that on such a night anything was possible. It was said that by the time we got there we would be too late to help as she was already about three hours late, but I said that it didn't matter we were going in any case.

Soon after the phone rang, and Les told me that they would like us to come, so off we went. Tom Buckley the Honorary Secretary went to the *Scillonian* at the pier to check that we got aboard all right and was (he told me) relieved to see our lights come on. As soon as we got to Peninnis Head I told the crew to strap themselves in, saying to the crew, 'Now we will see if this thing is any good or no.' I also asked Harry to inform Falmouth that we were leaving Peninnis Head at full speed. The wind and sea was about forty-five degrees on our Starboard bow and as soon as I opened the throttles we started to crash about, but I was determined to find out how good this boat was and so let her carry on. Soon after we passed the Eastern Islands, Bill says, 'The Decca position finder has packed up Matt,' this did not matter much as we had done many trips over these grounds, but I was hoping the radar would keep working, as it would be very useful when we got over to the land.

The boat was falling very heavily on to her shoulder and there was so much water flying over the wheelhouse windows that I could only get a glimpse of the sea in the light of the steering lights, every now and then. As we were getting over towards the land a bit Bill reported a contact on the radar, so I told him to put the curser on it. Every couple of minutes it was checked and it was found to be on the Starboard bow, we were now getting quite close. I was watching for lights and at last saw a white light and then it was gone. Next I saw a red light and said, 'There's her Port light,' but as I spoke I suddenly realised it was the Wolf Lighthouse. Being our first bad trip and with the weather on our shoulder I had expected her to make more leeway so we now turned towards the Runnel Stone, which after a while was picked up right ahead.

I was watching for the light which I saw every now and then but all of a sudden I again saw a red light very close, I realised that it was a ship and turned quickly to Starboard running down the side of a coaster or something within a stone's throw and then there was the Runnel Stone flashing again quite close. This ship's mast head light had got mixed up with the Runnel Stone Light as we were only seeing it every now and again on the top of a wave, we never did get a radar echo. The ship must have thought, 'What in the devil was that?' as we tore down her side at eighteen knots on a night like that.

We now eased down to search and I told Roy to tell me when we were a quarter of a mile off the shore by radar and I took over the steering from the top bridge. Brian came up with me to work the searchlight. On our second run we met the Lizard lifeboat, asking her to keep in touch by radio so that we knew all was all right with her, but soon after she was told to return to Newlyn for the night. We spotted something in the water inside of us, just off Lamorna and went in to check it but it turned out to be some fenders with something heavy still fast. As we were now quite close in and beam on to the sea I decided that these were not of any importance as we now knew the boat was lost so we carried on.

Later in the morning all the fishing boats came out searching, we tried to pick up one body but it kept slipping out of the lifting strap, then a helicopter dropped a diver and they winched it up. At about four o'clock we were told to call off our search so we went in to Newlyn to refuel, and get a cup of tea and a feed at the Seaman's mission. We were ready to set off for home when the coastguard asked us to go over to St. Michael's Mount because a helicopter had reported wreckage there. We towed what turned out to be a big piece of the stern of the *Solomon Browne* back to Newlyn. To see the wording 'Penlee Lifeboat' on the wreckage brought home more than ever what had happened, having known most of the crew. We then returned home receiving a signal of thanks from the Penlee station by radio on the way.

When we went into the engine room at Newlyn we found that the whole place was white with dried salt, from the deckhead to the bilge including the engines. This was caused on the trip over the night before with the water going up the air intakes and then being blown aboard everywhere, and then being dried out during the day by the heat of the engines. When we got home I rang the engineer inspector asking what we should do, he said that he was open to suggestions, as they had never had this problem before. We then decided for Bill and I to heat up fresh water and with plenty of soap, syringe the whole lot down then wash off the soap with warm water, making sure to get in around all the engine parts etc. We then dried her out by running the engines for an hour or two. This worked and we had no trouble at all afterwards.

We had another very sad occasion to deal with on July 16th 1983. This time we had the reserve lifeboat *Sir Max Aitken* on station and around mid-day the coastguard had reported that the air controller had lost contact with the B.A. helicopter, with twenty-six people on board, the last contact being three miles to the East. It was thick fog; I gave the phone to Pat saying, 'Get them quick it's the helicopter.' I ran straight out of the door meeting a van, which took me to the boathouse, and we were under way in six minutes. I controlled her from the bridge until we got to Bar Point then I went on the radar with Roy controlling on the bridge. On getting towards Toll's Island I could see a couple of echoes South of Deep Point but on checking them out they both turned out to be yachts. I had told the crew to get the rubber dinghy ready to launch, expecting to find the helicopter afloat so that we could take off the people, then tow the aircraft in. We now turned Eastwards still at full speed, depending on the radar.

I then noticed a shimmer on the set that I knew was not anything solid but I made up my mind to check it out, so told Roy to alter course to the South. Within a short time Roy said that the lookouts on the bow could smell paraffin, I then changed places again with Roy and eased the speed by about half. Soon after we saw people in the water with wreckage right ahead, as we closed them I eased down but when I put the engines into neutral, the Starboard one did not seem to come out of gear. I tried again quickly with no result, we were now nearly on top of them and to make her turn faster I put them both ahead and turned hard to Port going straight past. I then turned hard to Starboard back to them trying to get the engines into neutral gear again, but having to stop the engines altogether in between the two groups of people that were just a few yards apart.

The dinghy was launched with Harry and James aboard to pick up those on the Port side, while we picked up those on the Starboard side of the lifeboat. I had already asked Bill to go below and try to find out what was wrong with the engines. We now found that we had picked up six survivors, two children, two women and two men, as soon as we saw them in the water we had informed the coastguard of the position and that we were picking up survivors. One of the women, Megan Smith from St. Agnes was in a bad way, but the others told us that they were the only ones to get out of the helicopter when it crashed into the water. I asked Harry and James to take up, and keep in a position just in sight of us on our Port side, abeam so that we could cover twice the search area in the immediate vicinity.

We could hear the searching helicopter and because we were worried about Megan, we called him asking if his Doctor could be winched down to us. He agreed, but now the helicopter was having a job to find us even with V.H.F. directions. I then asked that if we directed him clear of us and then fired a flare straight up in the air, would that help. The visibility was better higher up, so with his agreement this was done. He saw the flare and shortly after was dropping through the fog over head and the Doctor was quickly dropped aboard.

After an examination he then advised me that it was necessary to get Megan to hospital right away, we had searched around the area, also we had been told by the other survivors that there was no-one else, so we headed for St. Mary's. On meeting the fishing boat *Swan Dancer* that was coming out to search we asked him to drop a Dhan Buoy to mark the position of the wreckage.

After landing everyone we returned to the search area, there were many local boats now arriving, and the fog had lifted a little but was still thick. The boatmen agreed to line up each side of the lifeboat at visibility distance from each other and let us control the search with their help by radio. This worked quite well and we were covering a very wide area. In one sweep some wreckage was picked up but this had drifted by the tide from the original position, the Penlee lifeboat joined us during our search and took position on the seaward end. The coastguard, after several hours called the search off, thanking everyone and asking us to stay in position until the arrival of a Naval salvage vessel to point out the position of the Dhan Buoy to them.

When the salvage ship arrived later that evening I led him to the Buoy and I also told him that in my opinion that was not the position of the crash. He smartly told me that he already knew where the helicopter was; some divers in a fishing boat had dragged a wire sweep and had found her. I knew this was not the helicopter that they had found but a bank of muddy sand. The ship then told me that as they knew where she was, we were no longer required, and so could return to St. Mary's. So to myself I said, 'And bugger you too,' and we returned to St. Mary's.

That evening a police sergeant and detective from Penzance came to see me to get a statement, after taking down the statement we were just chatting when one of them said that the salvage ship had not yet found the crashed helicopter. I just remarked, 'No, and they never will where they are searching,' one of them then asked, 'Why not Matt? Don't you agree with where they are looking?' I replied, 'I would have started searching three quarters of a mile East North East of that position'. They had no luck all the next day, but late that evening I had a call from the M.O.D. in London, 'I believe you don't agree with where the salvage vessel is searching,' to which I replied that I certainly did not. This chap then (I could tell by his voice that it was nearly choking him) asked me where I thought it was. I then told him the same thing as I had told the Police (who no doubt had passed it on in the first place) but I also made it quite

Landing helicopter survivors.

clear that I could not say that the helicopter was actually in that position, but that was the area I would start searching.

The next morning at 6 am the salvage vessel was told to shift her position to a position three quarters of a mile East North East of the Dhan Buoy, after doing this I was told that their divers had gone down just about on top of her. Another Naval ship that was involved showed me the positions on his chart and confirmed it, but no-one either from the salvage vessel, the M.O.D. or the Naval office had the good manners to even acknowledge me or say a brief thank-you – so much for common courtesy. I was told however, that I was referred to by name in the House of Commons and recorded in the Hansard records for all time.

Torrey Canyon.

Fastnet yacht 'Victride'.

CHAPTER 8

A NEW ERA

IN 1981 WE had a big change on the station – the *Guy and Clare Hunter* was replaced by a bigger and much faster, also more comfortable boat the *Robert Edgar*. She was one of the Arran class, something after the style of the Air Sea Rescue boats that I had been on when in the R.A.F. but not as big or as fast. The boat was a gift from Mr. and Mrs. A. Edgar and at Mrs. Edgar's request, as she was unable to travel to Scilly but wanted to christen the boat herself, some of us went up to Poole to the R.N.L.I. Headquarters to attend the christening.

There was also a big change in the crewing of the boat. There were now new rules on the age of retirement which was reduced to the age of fifty-five and everyone had to pass a medical. Some of the mechanics and coxswains were allowed to carry on until they reached the normal retirement age of sixty. It did not affect us too much as we had the slipway hands to take over from those that finished. Bill was already in Poole getting the boat ready and so Rodney, Brian, Ritchie and myself went up for the trials etc. Rodney Ward, Chairman of our local branch of the R.N.L.I. and Tom Buckley who was now Honorary Secretary also went up with us for the christening. When we arrived there was someone from Headquarters to meet Rodney and Tom, but no one for us. Bill was supposed to be there but we knew what Bill was like, and thinking he was late as usual the others went off to their posh hotel and we waited for Bill. In the end, after a lot of wise cracks especially from Ritchie and Brian we decided to walk from the station down to where we were supposed to sleep. We eventually found the place, after they had decided I should be pushed in a wheelchair for a while, which they thought was a great joke – I think this was referring to the new retirement age!

When we arrived at our lodgings there was no one there to tell us about rooms or anything, the Landlord of the pub next door who was supposed to own both houses did not know anything about us either. Now came a lot of wise cracks especially from Ritchie who was a right comedian with Brian not far behind. I said, 'Right we'll go up to Rodney's and Tom's hotel and let them sort it out.' There were two young ladies at the reception of the hotel and so I asked if they had a Mr. Ward and Mr. Buckley there. 'Just wait a moment I will see if I can find them,' was the reply from one of them and off she went. After a minute she came back to say that they were having their dinner so she couldn't disturb them. By this time I was getting steamed up and walking towards the door she had used said, 'Well if you won't, I will.' She then decided she would, so off she went – the boys were loving this bit of diplomacy! The man from the R.N.L.I. staff now arrived, so I explained the situation gradually working up steam and ending with, 'If somebody does not do something about it right away, we are on the next train home.' Funnily enough this brought action with phone calls etc. and soon the sheepish looking culprit Bill arrived. He always had more excuses than any Prime Minister but they were given in such a way that one could only grin and call him a few choice names, hinting that it was not quite the truth and then forget it.

We had a good four days or so out in the boat, and while ashore it was like a school holiday. The time came for us to set off home; if I remember right our first stop was Weymouth, again I was to be the centre of the joke of the evening. We were taken firstly to a brewery pub where everyone was invited to have a drink, mine was the usual soft drink, but while I was standing by the bar amongst the rest, glass in hand talking to one of the local lifeboat crowd, there was a flash of a camera and I was caught on camera in the pub drinking. It was a local news reporter who no doubt had been in on the joke – it was a set up and the photograph appeared in the local newspaper the next morning much to everyone's delight. The next day we did a towing exercise, towing the local lifeboat, to us this was a great laugh as we had towed more boats than some tugs. We also did an exercise with a Sea King helicopter, where we in turn were winched up, then landed back aboard. Of course they thought that I should be first to try it, but for all that I think we all reckoned it was great fun.

The next stop was over to Jersey, Guernsey and Alderney returning to Plymouth, where Les Vipond took us all home, where his wife Val had a nice meal waiting for us all. We then did a night trip home, calling at Fowey, just to see what the boat would be like in the dark. We arrived home on the 1st of July 1981. The following day we went up to Bristol with some of the other crewmembers to give them a chance to use the new equipment and to give the engines a good run in. On the way we called in at Ilfracombe, also went alongside the steel lifeboat anchored off Clovelly, but did not stop long because she was rolling quite badly but we could not allow anyone to say that we would not go alongside and moor up. Before we got to Bristol we received a call from I think it was Barry coastguard, asking us to take part in a search in that area. It was called off after an hour or so; we then went on and arrived in the early evening.

The next day we were open ship and I had the good luck of having an old R.A.F. mate, Dutchie Holland aboard for a look around, also chatting about the things aboard this boat that we would have loved to have had when we were in the crash boats, as we called them. We left that evening arriving home and ready for service the day after, when we said goodbye to the *Guy and Clare Hunter*, which went into the reserve fleet. When the Penlee Lifeboat the *Solomon Browne* was lost, the *Guy and Clare Hunter* was sent to Mousehole in her place. It was heard said in Mousehole that they were pleased to have 'Matt's boat' at their station.

Richard and George had now finished on the lifeboat and our main crew were, Roy, Bill, Harry, Rodney, Brian, Roy Duncan and myself, with several young spare crew, Derek, Colin and Peter who had been slip hands for some time, joined by James, Ritchie, Stuart and others. We sometimes took extra crew so that they would get experience of the equipment.

I have had many invitations to attend different functions over the years, many of which I would have attended but lots of times it was not possible from a place like Scilly, but there was one invitation that I accepted without hesitation. This was to represent the R.N.L.I. at the Festival of Remembrance at the Albert Hall. Pat and I had always watched it on the television and anyone who had been in the Services had a special interest, so I considered this a real honour. Pat and the girls went with me. I never felt at all nervous to march on my own behind four Merchant seamen (a service that I greatly admired) across the floor in front of the Queen and other members of the Royal Family plus all the audience, my thoughts were miles away from there I'm sure.

One of the next services we did in the *Robert Edgar* was to a yacht the *Concherto*, which was reported to be in difficulties about twenty miles North of Round Island. We passed up through Tresco Channel with a freshening South to South West wind, which soon increased to gale force with a nasty following quarterly sea. We reached the reported position at 6.45 pm and together with *H.M.S. Polington*, a minesweeper, which had arrived we began a search.

The *Polington* obtained a V.H.F./D.F. bearing on the yacht, which he passed on to us and on following the bearing we came up to the *Concherto* at a quarter after seven. Her sails were all stowed and the rudder seemed to be askew, she had a crew of two in the cockpit, the wind had now risen to force ten and the yacht was wallowing about badly. A large Finnish tanker had arrived and offered to give us a lee while we connected a towline, after connecting up we set off for home. At this time we had been listening to some other wireless signals, which indicated that there was another yacht in trouble to the East of us. The Sennen lifeboat was searching; also the *Polington* was heading to join in the search without result. I was very concerned about this and more so about the two men aboard the *Concherto* because of the weather and the way she was behaving. As darkness was not far away I decided that we must take the two men aboard by stopping the lifeboat and letting the *Concherto* drift down to lee slowly as we were shortening in the tow. Suddenly she made a lurch on a wave, with her bow coming in over the top of our rails toward the stern and hitting the side of the lifeboat's cabin bouncing off and running up the steps to the after deck. Luckily the crew had scattered very smartly and none were hurt, we were also rolling quite a lot, so she then slid off back into the water.

Eventually we got her alongside again and they jumped on to our side, with our crew grabbing them to get them on board. I was looking over the side of the bridge windscreen watching and trying to keep the lifeboat in position. After they had got aboard I could see that one of them still had his safety harness clipped to the yacht's mast stay which was going to pull him overboard. I shouted but they had seen it and James, leaning over our rail grabbed the yacht's stay as she was rolling towards us and quickly unclipped it. After getting them aboard I told the owner that if they did not find this other yacht soon I would have to cast his boat adrift to go join the search. He without hesitation says, 'That's all right, let it go now, I understand,' but I told him I would give it another half an hour. Shortly after the towrope parted, so I decided 'that's it' and set off at full speed for the other position. Eventually the other French yacht was spotted by the coastguard close inshore at Penzance, so we turned for home arriving at one the next morning after what originally looked like an easy little job, a vellum was awarded for this service.

We now had a new Honorary Secretary – again a local Doctor, Doctor Davis. We had a short service to find a local fishing boat, which we towed in on April the 2nd 1983 at 4.25 am but three and a half hours later we were called out again to a French ferry the *Armorique*, which had reported a fire aboard. We met up with her about ten miles North of Pendeen and she was now making for Newlyn at eighteen knots. As this was our own full speed we escorted her in to Mount's Bay. The Sennen and Penlee lifeboats arrived when she anchored, taking off the injured passengers, also with the help of helicopters. As we were told that we were no longer needed we returned to St. Mary's arriving at 3.15 pm.

Jean gave us our first grandchild, a girl on the 7th of July 1983, Jemma was a lovely baby and many of the fishermen from Newlyn would remember me bringing her down to see the boats on my shoulders as a little girl.

1983 was our busiest year; there were fifteen recorded lifeboat services without the unrecorded trips, most of them I cannot remember much about. They were the usual mixture of fishing boats, yachts and medical calls usually landing of injured or sick men, some of which could be quite a job in bad weather. There was one Spanish trawler I do remember, not for the weather which was quite reasonable, also the trawler was not many miles away but we took out the Doctor at about ten or eleven o'clock and after treating the man the Doctor came back aboard and we set off for home. Before we got there we had to go back again, the ship had told the Doctor by radio that something had gone wrong, we then brought the man ashore to hospital where he was treated, then with the Doctor we returned him to his ship. We had hardly got home before the Doctor, full of apologies to us, had to go back to the ship again to see this man. He then decided that this time after landing him he was staying in hospital. The Doctor was upset about all the messing about, but we knew it was not his fault and he was missing his night in bed just as we were. There was a lot of wise cracks and advice for him from the crew on the way back and forth.

When I was due to finish with the lifeboat I was caught out properly. We were sat down to dinner when the phone rang. It was Les our District Inspector; he wanted me to come to London to attend a meeting about co-operation between lifeboats and helicopters. My immediate reaction was that I did not want to come. He then said that there would be two other coxswains, a Naval pilot and an Air Force pilot taking part, but up to then we were the only boat that had taken part in real life-saving operations with helicopters, therefore the Head Office people would like me to be there. I was still not very keen, but at that point our daughter Lucy quickly butts in, 'What is it?' and after telling her, she persuades me to say that I would ring Les that evening, after I had thought it over. As soon as I dropped the phone they all started on me, telling me I should go. Lucy then told me that I should be ashamed of myself because I had made a fuss about the wireless communications between the helicopters and the lifeboats, when operating very close overhead, but now that they were giving me a chance to help put it right I just would not bother. Lucy knew this would make me feel ashamed and as if I was afraid to put my arguments to the test, so when I rang that evening I agreed to go up for this one night. I said that I would go to the meeting and then return straight home. Les then suggested that I could bring Pat with me, she could go around the big stores with one of the girls from the office while I was at the meeting, then I could meet her after lunch at the boat show, again I said I didn't want to see any yachts as we saw plenty at home. Now he told me that they would like Admiral Graham to present the vellum I had been awarded for the service to the B.A. helicopter at the boat show. I was now in a corner, but after insisting that we could still catch the night train home, it was all agreed.

Soon after I began wishing that I had not agreed to any of it, but having said I would, no way could I now change my mind. Lucy, Jean and Pat must have been greatly relieved, because they of course knew what was on the cards. Most of it was done through Lucy, while at work in the bank, using code words etc. like M.I.5 I was afterwards told.

When the morning came for Pat and me to leave for London on the helicopter, it was thick fog so I said, 'Well that's it we can't go now,' but I was soon told, 'well you will have to go by boat instead,' and off we went. Unbeknown to me Pat was now worried sick about all the others that were coming by the later helicopter, but not knowing what was going on I had none of the worries. Heather one of the R.N.L.I. staff was there to meet us at Paddington; she then took us to a small hotel on the outskirts, where we had been booked in. Next morning a car picked me up to take me to the meeting, it turned out to be a good meeting and possibly did some good from the communications side. After the meeting one of the R.N.L.I. staff nearly gave the game away while we were waiting for the car to take us to lunch he turned to me saying, 'You're happy about Les looking after the boat while you are away then Matt', in my innocence I just said, 'Les isn't looking after the boat, Roy is'. 'Oh yes, of course he is,' he replied, so it just passed off.

We went to the boat show where we met Pat, the vellum was presented and we were on our way out. I had just said to Pat, 'Well thank God that's all over, we can get some fish and chips and catch the train home', when the next thing I knew a big chap stopped me amongst the crowd saying, 'You are Matt Lethbridge aren't you?' Like a fool I thought, 'I know that face, it's Eamonn Andrews,' but I still did not realise what was happening. In Scilly we have seen so many famous people over the years that it just seemed natural. Then I noticed a camera appear over his shoulder, the red book appeared and of course he says, 'Matt Lethbridge, This Is Your Life'. From then on I did not see anyone but my guard and Eamonn himself. I was taken off in a big car, on asking, 'Where was Pat?' they said not to worry she was being looked after and I would see her later. On arrival at the theatre I was taken into a room where my guard looked after me, the make-up girl then arrived but I refused her help point blank!

Eamonn and myself then walked up to the stage through the audience. It was funny to find that I was not at all nervous because one or two people touched my hand as I walked along, people that had been to Scilly on holiday most likely, and so I just felt awfully embarrassed, wondering what in the devil they were going to say when we got on the programme. When I turned and looked at the audience I again was surprised to find that owing to the lights facing us I could not really see much more than the first row.

As the programme started I now was more interested and worried about what was going to be said, also I was wondering who I would meet again possibly from my Air Force days, but as the time went on I now just did not really think of it as a show at all. It seems stupid but to me it seemed as if I was just being told a story about what had happened to all these people. I again met up with Pat, Jean and Bob, and Lucy first, then Harry and Pam, Richard and June, also Roy, Bill and Rodney, from the lifeboat crew. This was also when Jean was talking about Jemma and they showed a pre-recorded film of her. It was lovely; she was in her bouncer enjoying herself off stage.

The programme was made up of lifeboat jobs really, but it was nice to meet the people from the helicopter accident, the Fastnet yachts, the I.T.N. members from the *Braemar*, the Captain of the *Nordanhav* and it ended with the two children Howard and Helen who were both orphaned by the helicopter crash. At the end of the programme my brother George appeared on his crutches, he had just had a leg (up to his knee) removed three weeks before, but had been flown home from New Zealand. It was the first time he had been home since he left thirty-four years before. We then had a party that evening with all involved and many others, family and friends, before returning home the next day.

The last service trip for me was in July 1984 I remember there was quite a mix up over the position; it was originally given as twelve miles and I believe it was about 70 degrees from Peninnis Head. There were several changes in the boat's crew, Roy had finished the year before and Rodney was the second coxswain, with Barry Bennett ready to take Rodney's place when I finished and Rodney would take mine.

The call was to a yacht called the *Wild Goose*, I can't remember what the trouble was but it was quite good weather and it was reported to the coastguard by a tanker that had it moored to their stern. Just for practice I asked Barry to plot it on the Decca chart, this was about 85 degrees from Crow Sound. I was expecting to see the ship as soon as we got clear of the land and could not understand why we could not, but we carried on. We did see another tanker in a similar direction but a lot farther away and so went towards it. I then questioned the position and asked for a latitude and longitude position. As soon as I got the reply '51 degrees North' I knew something was really wrong and replied to that effect. Again I was assured it was right until I reminded the sender that this position was at the least sixty miles away and so told him that I would ask the ship myself. The poor chap forgot that he had his transmission button on and I heard him say, 'Bugger it, that bloody man is right again.' So I thought that this was a very good way to finish.

I retired from the lifeboat on 20th January 1985 after being coxswain for just twelve weeks short of thirty years and just short of forty years in the boat. I had taken over from my Dad who had taken over from my Grandfather as coxswain covering a period of over seventy-one years between us.

On my 61st birthday I had a great retirement party arranged for me with many presents, and framed letters from the crews and committees etc. There was also many of the past crew members, other coxswains and inspectors, most of them having their wives with them. The then retired R.N. Admiral Graham who had been captain of the Air Craft Carrier *Ark Royal* before retiring and was at this time top man at R.N.L.I. headquarters also came down for it.

The highlight of the speeches etc. was when it came to my turn to reply. I borrowed my (future) son-in-law Ken's crutches (he had had an accident and had a broken leg at the time), I also borrowed Pat's glasses, I then stuck an ear plug in my ear with wire attached and hobbled up to the mike. After thanking everyone etc. I then told them that as I was not much good at speeches, I had recorded something and would play it for them. I switched on the cassette recorder, which now played the song 'Oh Lord it's hard to be humble, when you're perfect in every way'. This caused a real good laugh and end to my service.

One evening I had a very great surprise, the doorbell rang, on answering it was Wendy Hick from St. Agnes. She gave me a small package in which was a lovely wrist watch on the back of which was engraved the words 'Matt from St. Agnes 20–1–85'. Wendy then told me that this was a thank-you from all the inhabitants of St. Agnes, men, women and children, in fact every person on the Island had contributed to it. This will always be something special.

I was still fishing and quite fit, I missed the lifeboat trips for a while, as strange as it may seem, I loved to drive the boats at full speed regardless of the weather having absolute confidence that handled properly the lifeboats would take it and the crews would have to. I had never eased a boat down when proceeding on a service, no matter what the strength or direction of wind or sea. Many people have asked, 'What was the worst trip you had, as regards to weather?' I don't think I can even now answer that, winds of over one hundred miles an hour had been recorded, not by us, also wave measurements of sixty-five feet by wave recorders, but I can honestly say that as soon as I got aboard the boat it never seemed as bad as I thought it might be. It was always a dirty, a nasty or a rotten old night and blowing about nine or ten, as far as I was concerned. I was lucky that I have never been seasick in my life and was able to manage without sleep for long periods, I never slept on a long service regardless of time taken.

Shark drowned in my fishing gear.

Yachting in the 'Braemar'.

CHAPTER 9

OTHER STORIES

I HAVE HELPED to salvage many boats, yachts and other vessels over the years, but there was one that gave me special satisfaction, it was refloating the local motor launch *Tean*, a fifty-two foot cargo launch that had broken adrift from her moorings one night during a bad Westerly gale. The next morning she was found ashore on the corner of the beach and rocks under Beachfield House. She was badly holed and had severe damage to her keel; also she was broadside on to the beach with the sea breaking over her. In the morning the manager of the Steamship Co. asked me if I would take over the job of trying to get her off on the afternoon tide. I was a bit surprised at this as I thought that they had men on their own firm that may not like me taking charge, but he assured me that they would give me all the assistance they could if I was willing to try this job, which at the time looked just about hopeless.

As soon as the tide allowed, the shipwrights started cutting away some of the rough planks around the big holes in the *Tean's* bottom, while some of us got a big anchor of mine, also a long coil of four inch rope, a three fold block and tackle plus some other shackles and gear. We all then helped the shipwrights while they patched the holes with felt or rubberoid and sheets of thin plywood. At low water we dug in the anchor as far down the beach as we could get in good holding ground, the four inch rope was made fast round the anchor with the other end through a fairlead at the stern of the *Tean*. We then fastened the standing block to the mooring post in the bow while the moving block was made fast the anchor cable aft and the hauling part around the anchor winch forward. While Les, Bob, Alf and Frank had been working on the boat, Henry and Ernie had been working on the engine, Clifford and myself got the rest ready with some help from the others when needed.

As the tide started getting round the boat all we could do was to shelter in the wheelhouse while the waves smashed against the side, sending the spray flying, it was still a gale of wind with heavy sea. As the *Tean* started to move and bang up and down on the bottom we kept heaving on the winch, then on a big sea she turned over on to the other bilge so the seas were now breaking right aboard. After a while her stern was moving to seaward but as she started to lift on each sea she also was moving towards the rocks. I then asked Henry to start the engine, at first he complained that the coolers would get full of sand, until I reminded him that if he didn't he would not have any engine. I then went full ahead on to the beach, with the helm hard to Port, this then helped to pull her stern in to the wind as they tightened up on the stern rope. As she lifted on each sea, now she started to jump astern, I then went full astern while they kept heaving on the rope and off she came.

While all this was going on the *Scillonian* was parting her mooring ropes at the pier so the quay hands were busy mooring her. After we re-floated the *Tean* we kept going astern taking in the anchor rope until there was room to swing her round, bow to the sea, she was now under control, so after cutting the rope we headed for the old pier. I think the Steamship management were not so pleased that we had re-floated her, and had not really expected it to happen, but knew that it would look better if they could say that I had failed than saying that they had failed to try and save her – now they were faced with a massive repair job. We had five pounds each for the job but I was quite happy thinking, 'Well, you shouldn't have asked should you?'

Some time after while the *Tean* was up on the top of the beach being repaired we had a bad gale and the lifeboat was needed. It was dark and as we ran down the slipway she made a sudden lurch to Starboard, jumping out of the keelway and going out over the side of the slip. We found out after that one of the big wood wedges had been washed from under the *Tean* with the gale early in the evening and had rested in the keelway with the thin end up so the lifeboat had just shot right up over it and over the side – again we had been very lucky to have no damage.

The next special thing I can think of was one day when I was hauling a string of ten pots, which I had shot very close along some rocks. There was not much wind but it was blowing on to the rocks, my weather end buoy rope had gone ashore and so I had to haul from the lee end against a strong tide, there was also quite a bit of swell in the water. I had hauled the pots and was pulling in the buoy rope intending to cut it if it did not pull clear. As the swells came in they pushed the boat towards the rocks each time and I had put my engine into astern gear, but was not getting the results I expected. I gave the engine more power while still pulling in the rope but by now I was really close to the rocks. When I gave the engine full power this caused a whining screaming noise, which I thought was from the gear box, and I jumped aft to start my other engine, but the next swell threw the bow of the boat in over some rocks and there she stayed. After trying full astern on my other engine I looked over the stern of the boat seeing that there was a big bunch of something around the propeller, thinking it was weed I tried to pull it off but found there was no movement at all.

The boat was now twisting and creaking on every swell, and when I looked at the bow the wooden ends were coming away from the stem of the boat, which meant that she was splitting in half, long ways. On looking to see how far the split was, I found it was from under water at the forefoot widening to a gap of about three inches at the top, the water was now pouring in. I had a hand held V.H.F. set aboard so decided that I must jump onto the rock with the set to ask someone to take me off, because the boat was coming apart. Before I could clamber onto the foredeck another big swell lifted the boats bow and as the spare engine was still going astern off the boat came. Now I was worse off and thought of steaming back onto the rocks to make sure of saving myself but then decided to set the helm hard to Starboard with the engine in head gear slow, getting rid of the pots by just throwing them overboard. The water of course was still pouring in up to the bottom boards or plats, which were floating around.

I then heaved up the ballast of iron half hundred weight pegs and big lumps of iron, after having lifted them on to the after engine house, I then placed them near the stern, lifting the bow of the boat up quite a bit. I was now just about clapped out, but on seeing that the water was not coming in quite as bad I started bailing with a bucket – this was nearly killing me but I could see that I was very slowly gaining on it, I also knew that the more I got out, the less would come in because of the boat becoming lighter in the water. After a lot of bailing (and a lot of sweat, which must have added to the water level) I knew that I had it beat as long as the boat held together. After some time I decided that as long as I kept bailing and nothing else went wrong, I would make it as far as St. Agnes if I were lucky. When I reached St. Agnes I had trimmed the boat a bit more and made for home, on reaching the harbour I drove straight in on to the beach.

When the tide went back I found that the cause of all my trouble was that while I had been hauling my pots the tide had drifted a big bundle of half-inch wide flat nylon packing case strips onto my propeller, thereby making it useless. This shows that some careless act of dumping at sea can cause possibly a loss of life to someone else. On pulling the boat up for repair the next day we found that there was not a mark of any sort, not even a scratch anywhere on her bottom. There were two marks on the sides of her bow, one on each where she had been jammed between the rocks but as we pulled her out of the water, the water was pouring out of the bottom planks through all the twisting while on the rocks. Nevertheless, with the help of the Cornish Fishermen's Society and Peter Martin the boat builder we had her re-nailed and the stem repaired, so I was back fishing in her in about seven to ten days. Brian who was in the lifeboat with me helped me haul my pots while this work was going on and on return from hauling both his and my gear, I would help Peter working on the boat, I was soon ready to go again.

Lucy our second daughter was married to Ken Wilkins on the 12th of June 1987. Ken was in the Police Force and so at this time we lost Lucy to the mainland, but thankfully not too far away, near enough that we are able to visit each other once or twice a year.

One visit was to see our second lovely granddaughter Rebecca, born on the 19th March 1988, another lovely girl to try to spoil as much as we could get a chance to.

I had now become an old age pensioner and as I had always stated that the day I picked up my pension was to be the day I finished fishing for a living, I kept that promise. I had enjoyed being my own boss all my life, doing the work that I had loved since I was a boy, answerable only to myself during good and bad seasons. During those years I had many different good jobs offered to me. I was offered a job as skipper of the *Braemar* to go cruising down to the Mediterranean at one time. Another time when the *Scillonian II* arrived in Scilly my uncle was one of the crew that was on her trip down from the builders yard but on arrival he had a bad cold and so was unable to do the next trip or two across to Penzance and back. So I was asked to take his place, and so for that period I was now a seventy-year-old seaman using Uncle Jim's discharge book. When the shipping master saw the discharge book it was so old that he'd never seen the likes of before. I remember Captain Daniels while I was taking my trick on the wheel, trying to persuade me to pack up fishing and stay on with him, but this offer and many others did not even tempt me. It was hard work with very long hours, at times sixteen to eighteen hours a day, and many times when a lifeboat job had turned up I would go forty-eight hours or more without sleep, but I enjoyed both jobs so it was well worth it.

We were again delighted when in 1990 Lucy and Ken gave us another lovely baby, this time a boy to be named Thomas Charles Matthew, the Charles being a family name of Ken's, so now we had three lovely kids to help keep us from getting old too fast.

I was intending to do many of the things that I had not had time to do before, now that I was able, but this did not work out. In 1995 I suffered a bad heart attack and was again taken to Penzance hospital, this time by a Royal Navy Sea King helicopter from Culdrose. I was on a stretcher and when the winch man bent down to pick me up, he suddenly recognised me from one of the lifeboat jobs when he was winched down to us. More or less the same thing happened at Penzance, when the hospital porter picked up the stretcher, and when the heart specialist came to see me although I had never seen him or he me, we both recognised each other through Doctor Bell's stories and descriptions of each other. Mr. Gibbons became a good friend of mine while I was under his care. After being allowed home again I was only home a short time (about a week), when I had another stretcher trip on the local helicopter with the same trouble.

I thankfully once more survived to return home, this time it was a slow job but with Pat's care, keeping a pretty close eye on what I was up to and many ticking offs for pushing myself over the limit, I am glad to say I got over it pretty well again.

Jean and Bob got divorced in 1990, but in 1993 Jean met John Goody, son of Jess and Anne Goody who she had been out with when she was eighteen years old, and in 1996 they were married and live just across the road from us.

My Grandfather was coxswain of the lifeboat when the then Prince of Wales had his first trip in a lifeboat in 1920. The present Prince of Wales had his first trip in a lifeboat in the *Guy and Clare Hunter*, down the same slipway in 1977 when I was coxswain. I have had the honour of meeting many of the Royal Family from Grandmother to great grandchildren. Pat and I also attended a cocktail party on board the *H.M.Y. Britannia*, where I was able to talk with Her Majesty about the *Torrey Canyon*. We had previously been presented on the pier with the lifeboat crew.

One summer the Duchess of Kent with her two young sons came out with us in the *Robert Edgar* one evening to watch the gig race. It had been arranged with the harbour master that we would embark them at the pier a while before the race was due to start. We went out for a short trip around and I could see the St. Agnes gig coming to take part in the race so I headed towards her. The Duchess and the two boys were on the bridge and I had been telling them that this gig, the *Shah* was the last gig to be used in earnest for pilotage, when I could remember her being used to attend the dredger *Foremost* with the lifeboat. I also told them that the man steering the *Shah* was the son of that same pilot. We were now quite close alongside when the coxswain of the gig looked up and shouts, 'Who's that BIRD you've got up there with you Matt?' You should have seen his face when he realised just who it was!

I have also been very fortunate in meeting many well known people, some famous, some not, some very interesting and nice people, others who were full of their own importance but in truth quite ignorant and of no importance to anyone other than themselves. I detest snobbery and have found over the years that in general these sorts of people really amount to nothing. The nice people to know are those that are interesting to listen to but who are also interested in listening to what oneself has to say.

I remember one morning being in the carpenter's shed waiting for a haircut, the carpenter was an ex-ship's chippie and he used to cut hair for the crew when he was at sea, so after persuasions he became well known for a quick trim on a Saturday morning.

On this particular morning, Mr. Ray Gunter who was a Minister at the time for the Labour Government, was also waiting for a haircut, he and I had a great friendly argument. When I arrived home Pat wanted to know what I was arguing with Ray Gunter about. I asked how she knew that I had even seen Ray Gunter, and she said that she had been to the shop where he was telling them that he had spent a great morning arguing with Matt. On being asked who won he replied, 'Well I believe he did really'.

On the opposite side of the coin however, I remember on one occasion asking a Minister of Education some awkward questions at a public meeting. When I next put up my hand he said, 'I am not answering you anymore tonight, I've had enough of you,' to which I had the greatest of pleasure in informing him, that was fine as I was going to agree with what he was saying this time! That man in my book was a complete snob, too full of himself to be able to recognise it.

There was one M.P. I knew that never promised anything without trying his best to keep his promise. He was a real gent and when asking him to look into something or for his help, if he took out his little notebook you could depend on some action. This gent was a member of the R.N.L.I. committee for some years and was on the Island when we were out one very bad night. On hearing the lifeboat rockets he made his way to the boathouse, we had already left. After a while the call was cancelled but Land's End Radio could not get in touch with us to re-call us for some time. When we returned he was still in the boathouse, I then told him that we had for some time been trying to get a wireless transmitter and receiver set for the coastguard station. They themselves had also been trying but could make no progress; he then took out his little book and shortly after the set was installed.

I remember also one woman of the yachting fraternity that I met before she had written her story. This book to me was like reading something from Fairyland, especially knowing that she, a few years before when I first met her, had to have an instructor with her and even then lowered sail and used the engine to come to anchor. However, after one trip and a book she was now a greater sailor than Christopher Columbus – and a greater snob.

As I have already said I have no time for snobbery, on the following occasion I was tested to the limit. At one time in the late sixties or early seventies I believe, the *Scillonian II* was running Sunday trips, which meant that for a spell in the summer months we were getting our Sunday papers on Sunday instead of on Monday. It also meant that there was always a queue outside the paper shop, at times when I had been in this queue I had noticed a certain bloke who considered himself better than the rest of us, walk straight in disregarding the queue and come out with his papers. This was not pleasing me very much;

nevertheless my chance arrived one day when I was just inside the door when he arrived. I waited until the person that was serving placed his papers on the counter for him, and then I quickly nipped out of the queue and slapped my hand down on top of them. I then asked the shop assistant, 'Do I pay for my papers?' 'Yes' she replied. 'Do I pay the same price as he does?' I asked indicating to this bloke standing alongside me. 'Yes,' she answered. 'Was I here before him?' again the answer was, 'Yes.' 'Right,' I said,'Then I want my papers before him.' I then turned to the four or five people that had been ahead of me in the queue asking if they wanted theirs first, but they seemed struck speechless. So I was served with my papers and after thanking the girl, I then turned to the other bloke saying, 'And don't you ever try that again when I am in the queue.' I have referred to him as a bloke on purpose because his behaviour did not deserve any better. I must admit that it gave me a great deal of pleasure to put him in his place.

I also think many times of a Dutch yachtsman sailor, a gentleman of no position of importance or riches. We first met when we answered a call in the *Guy and Clare Hunter* from a ship, which had come across this man in a single-handed voyage from the West Indies to Holland. He had run out of food three or four days before and was on very short water rations. We met the ship that was standing by him, we then towed him into St. Mary's, and it was a Saturday night. Usually The Mission of Seaman's representative would see to any need of a seaman in trouble when we brought them in and so I took that for granted. On Sunday morning I went down to see the man, and after talking about his boat and his trip he asked if he could buy some food, as he hadn't any. I could hardly believe it, no one had been to see him! I then went home and got some food etc. for immediate use, and at the same time got hold of the Seaman's representative to get on with his job. Later talking to Jacob, as he was called he told me he was an ex-merchant seaman and he worked his way all over the world by using a battery radio and tuning in to the different broadcasting stations by turning his set around, and when he lost contact would steer by compass until he picked up the next radio signal. He had a sextant but did not like it much he said. He had been completely out of food, and down to a spoonful or two of water, but he still had his Life-raft rations complete, but would not touch them until in his words, he had to. He insisted in giving me four wood masks that he had from the West Indies, his mother was sick and he was going home to look after her.

This was the kind of man that was really worth listening to. His boat was no shining racer, it was a steel able looking boat, there were no modern aids, but everything had a place and everything was in it's place. His rigging, shackles etc. were well looked after, and of the right size, he was a quiet man, a real seaman.

Over the years I have had a lot of fun and a lot of clashes with authorities of one sort or another, but in general I don't think they ended with a vendetta or life-long upset. Some of my collisions with people were about unnecessary changes in Scilly, just for the sake of making more money, but at the same time making one more step on the road to ruining the greatest little place on God's earth. There are snags living on the Islands, but if one does not get their newspapers or are unable to buy certain things, so what? – it's not the end of the world.

I remember some years ago I was walking up the road, where I found that a wall was already being built to block off an opening for cars etc. leaving only a walkway. I had not seen any notice of this or heard anything, so went to see Mr. Mumford who was the Chairman of the Council at the time, and a family friend who had lived in the same street since at least 1927. I then asked him what was happening. He replied by telling me that it was to build an Old Folks Home. I then said that it should have been published for objections before blocking the opening and also that they could still build the home there without changing the opening. After a public enquiry etc. the plans were changed, the home was built in the same place and the opening is still there, and of much more importance now than it was at the time, and so I rest my case. However, I still believe a chance to have the best Old Folks Home in the world was missed by not using the Holgates Hotel site, which would have had a view of the whole harbour.

Another of what I like to believe was on the credit side of my arguments, was the forming of our local Fisheries Committee for the Islands. After being told it was impossible to have such a committee I threatened to form it myself, which I knew was possible by law. The Council then agreed, it took us about twelve years to get it passed, but again I believe it has saved a great part of the life and charm of Scilly.

I was also one of the founder members of the Environmental Committee, but even at the outset I could see that mainland interests would finally control it. Some other Islanders and myself tried to stop this happening, but money talks and now it is controlled by English Nature or some other English Heritage people that were neither born, brought up, or ever lived in Scilly. After having some promises broken to us I resigned from the original committee and remained able to speak my own mind.

After reading back over what I have just written it seems as if I was a bit of a nuisance. I suppose that maybe I was at times, but I remember a past clerk, and then Chairman of the Council, with whom I had many clashes in public meetings, came to see me when he was leaving Scilly to say good-bye and to tell me that with all our arguments and falling out at meetings, he knew that as soon as the meeting was over, we left what was said behind the door. This was, he said something he really appreciated. I must also say that with the many times I have asked to see officers of the Council or Duchy of Cornwall etc. I have always been able to, without trouble – sometimes even when it was known that I was on the warpath. Also it has been suggested to me by at least three different Islanders who were Chairman of the Council at the time, that I should put my name forward for election and they would sign my nomination papers, but my answer was always the same. 'When you can tell me that something passed in Council cannot be overruled by someone in London or elsewhere who knows nothing whatsoever about the Island life or the subject, then that would be the day to ask me again.' Sadly though most of what I have seen of meetings results in a lot of chatter and turns out to be a complete waste of time.

At least twice while out fishing I have found lost divers, once I was just going towards my next string of pots when I saw what looked like a bloke on a small rock, the Old Bess which is under water at high tide and was now about three feet high. Because there were no diving boats around I decided it must be a seal, the seal then started waving like mad so I changed my mind again and went over to him. I stopped right alongside the rock about three feet away from the side of the boat. He seemed to be in a right state about the boat having lost him, so I told him to jump in the water and I would help him aboard. There was no way he was going to get back in the water and so I had to watch my chance, then put the shoulder of the boat on the rock to allow him to get aboard without touching the water. After he was aboard I went in around other rocks and found the boat looking for him. As we got close there was obviously great relief with a lot of cheering and joking, but my passenger was very far from being amused and he certainly let them know. Now I think of it he himself even forgot to say 'thank-you', I wonder if he ever went diving again?

In general I had very little time for these Sub Aqua divers, at that time there was a lot of pot robbing going on, but it was a job to prove it. To anyone fishing for a living it was as clear as the nose on one's face and so another diver I found when I was on my way home one day (he also found how fond of them I was). I noticed one of the diving boats that was nowhere near any wreck that I knew of, he was also zigzagging about all over the place. He then headed over to meet me telling me that he had lost a diver, who should have surfaced at least thirty minutes or more before. I knew which wreck this boat usually worked on and the position of it, and so headed off in the direction of the tide, which was a different direction all together from where they were looking and after about twenty minutes I found him. It was reasonable weather and so I caught hold of his hands and asked him if he was all right, he told me that he was fine now that he had been found. I placed his hands on the gunwale of the boat saying, 'Well you hang on there until your mates come because I aren't having any divers aboard here.' I then beckoned to his mates to come over, when they saw that I had found him, they of course were again like the other lot, very relieved. The owner of the boat then said that the next time we are near you we will bring you up some crayfish. I replied that I did not want them to do it, so they said all right we will put some in your pots, by now I was again steamed up. I replied by telling them that if I knew they had done that I would throw the fish overboard and told them to keep clear of my bloody pots and to keep clear of me. I said that I didn't want any thanks and that I would pick up a dog if I found one swimming.

Another time some divers, I suppose on a training exercise from the Navy, had been here looking for the *Association* – this was in an area that I was always working. On seeing their vessel arrive one evening I went down to the quay to tell them that I had gear around the Gilstone, which was the rocks on which everyone knew the *Association* was wrecked in 1707, with much gold and silver etc. most of which was salvaged at the time, but there was still quite a lot left for those that could find exactly where she was. These particular divers had been searching for her for four years and they told me this would be their last year. I was afraid they might cut off my buoy ropes with the propellers and asked them what time in the morning they were starting. When told five o'clock because it was low water, I told them that that was no good because the Gilstone tide would be running hard, so I was hoping to get my gear before they arrived. I also told them that there were only two places that I thought the wreck would be because of the tides etc. also saying which one I thought the remains may be lying in. The next morning after getting some of my fishing gear I was rushing to get through them and to the Gilstone before they arrived but was not able. When I did get there they waved me over telling me that they had found three cannons but did not want the find broadcast until they had lifted them. Two or three days later they brought one of the cannons in, this made big news. Within a couple of days a Penzance man arrived with other divers, then they brought up the other cannons, which had not been marked, and from then on this man said he had found the wreck. He eventually claimed the sole rights of diving on it, bringing up a large number of coins over the years. It was hard luck on the Navy boys but I suppose there was some reason by law that they must have been unable to claim the rights themselves. I still have a newspaper cutting somewhere written by the skipper of the Naval boat stating how they had found it with the help of myself.

There was another couple of divers that I was sure at that time were bringing in quite a lot of lobsters, a lot of which were coming from around and out of my pots. One day they came alongside asking me if I would tell them where the trawler was that had hit rocks and sunk the winter before, which I had found after some information from Leonard Jenkins, who was another fisherman and old friend. I told the divers I would show them, not because I wanted to help them but because while they were robbing that, they were keeping away from my gear. As you will have guessed I had very little time for any of them, and as the saying goes, some of them would cheat their own Granny, given the chance.

Sadly, Bill died after having a heart attack a few years after retiring from the lifeboat. I was asked if I would say a few words at his funeral service, having known him better than anyone outside of his family. I was now faced with a problem – how could I talk about Bill at such a sad occasion without a smile? He was a bloke you couldn't even think of without smiling and such a likeable character that even when you knew he was giving you the biggest load of codswallop possible and you may feel exasperated, it was impossible to fall out with him. No matter what the weather was like, if the boat was needed he would be there and during his time with me there was never any engine or equipment trouble on our station boats. At the service I explained all of these things and then decided to tell a story of a time when we had a relief boat on the station. We had a call out but found that the port engine refused to start. After a few attempts I decided to launch on the one engine, hoping to start the port one while underway. As soon as we got off the slipway Bill was in the engine room trying to start the other engine. After getting clear of the harbour I looked down the hatch from the steering position to see Bill actually beating the offending engine with his cap! At the same time, although I could not actually hear what he was saying, I felt sure he was telling it that it had no parents and was made up out of spare parts! I jokingly told those in the wheelhouse that we may have to return to land Bill, but after the beating, the amazing thing was that when Bill poked himself halfway through the hatch and pressed the starting button again – low and behold the engine started, purring like a cat for the rest of the trip! After telling this story all the congregation were laughing, including his family, knowing this was the real Bill. Maureen, his wife, and other members of his family were very pleased with the way I had described him telling me that I could never have done it better, much to my great relief.

Very sadly, my brothers have also now all passed away and for the first time in well over eighty years there are none of the family connected with the lifeboat service in Scilly.

The 27th December 1999 was our Golden Wedding Day so partly because we had missed our first party, the girls reckoned that we deserved a bit of a do this time. I could in no way argue for once, so they fixed it all up, with Mum's help of course, to get all our families together, many of them coming from the mainland, also many of our close friends. We were sorry that there were many others who could not be with us because of the time of year. We had a great evening and I at the last minute managed to persuade Pat to once more after fifty years, have a quick waltz around the floor. We had many presents, also a lot of cards, and we are now looking forward to our Diamond Wedding party.

Over the years I have been lucky enough to make good friendships with visiting fishermen, many of these have lasted from fathers to sons etc., these friendships have been and still remain very important to me. A good example of this type of friendship is when I suffered my heart attack and was flown away to Penzance hospital. The day after while I was in intensive care I was surprised when two of these friends who were both trawler skippers charged in without anyone seeing them. They came to my bedside and one says, 'I thought I would come to see you because I'm going to sea at mid-day and I want to put my name on one of your paintings before you go on your 'journey' ', – meaning that if I was going to die, they wanted one of my paintings! The other then said, 'And I'm going to sea at six this evening and I want to do the same!' They were both grinning like Cheshire cats, even with the drips and monitors etc. I had to laugh at them that is until the nurse realised that they had got in to see me. I spent many hours with these sort of men, when they have been in for shelter or some other reason and I hope on some occasions I have been of some help to some of them, they are the salt of the earth.

I must admit without any shame that I had no nonsense with rules or rulebooks, people who don't know the job make most of them I reckon and I was always ignoring them. I remember when the *Guy and Clare* arrived there were no big oars aboard, where as the *Cunard* had four, so I took two of them and put them aboard the new boat. When the inspector came on his visit he said that I must send them back to the depot but I refused. He then informed me that it would not be possible to row a big boat like this with two oars, and also that she was twin engined. I let him know that I was not quite as stupid as that, but we might need them for fending off or something, even steering, and still refused. Some years after we were attending the wreck of a catamaran at the back of Tean, she was ashore in a narrow gully amongst the rocks and there was one man on the deck. The weather was reasonable so I told two of the chaps to take one of the oars and with one on each side hold her stern from hitting the rocks. The man wanted us to try towing her off but I told him it wasn't possible, he insisted so the tow rope was made fast the mizzen mast from our bow, he was taken aboard and we backed our way astern. When clear I said, 'O.K. make fast,' and we came astern with a bit of power. Part of the cat came off, including the mizzen mast and some of the rigging but the rest stayed behind. Where there is ignorance, there is bliss?

We also used the paddles sometimes for keeping the bow up while slipping in fine weather, much against the rules but very successful on each occasion.

On one occasion we were re-slipping the boat in a light wind, with only one head rope on the windward bow buoy and after backing straight in the channel way, we were being heaved up with the winch. I was told that I shouldn't do that. I honestly did not know what this chap meant, it was our normal procedure, but he said that we should have four lines, two at the bow and two at the stern. My answer was that if I could not put her back on the slip without all that palaver I would pack in and let someone else take over.

Another time we were on a normal exercise with an inspector, and when we used the emergency steering, the tiller kept pulling out of it's socket. As usual I then had a great argument about boring a hole down through the lot and dropping a big pin in it. I was told no, but we could have a hole side on with a drop nose pin, I then exploded, 'Who's going to be daft enough to be doing that especially in a gale of wind.' After he had gone back I bored a hole and made a nice pin with a small chain fastened to the tiller. The next time the same man came to do the exercise, he said, 'Rig the emergency steering,' so I told the crew to rig the emergency steering in an exasperated tone. I had already told them not to let him know what I had done, so they loved it. After rigging they reported, 'All rigged,' so I said, 'O.K. hard to Starboard' and around the boat came. The inspector who was standing beside me looked aft with a puzzled face, I then said, 'Hard to Port,' again everything was fine. He was expecting the tiller to fall out but could not understand why it didn't, so he went tearing aft, then came back very annoyed saying, 'Who did that?' My reply was, 'I did'. 'Who gave you permission?' he asked. 'No-one, but it bloody well works doesn't it?' The reply from a very disgruntled man, 'Well yes, it works', end of story.

I was not fond of exercises except exercising in the use of equipment carried on the boat and as long as the crew knew how to use it I could see no sense in making up imaginary situations. I found that every service or rescue was different and called for different action, and that action could only be taken on the spur of the moment by people who were dealing with and making these decisions in their normal working life.

I know one time when on one exercise, this particular chap decided that we should learn how to recover a man overboard situation. The idea was a typical, big ship exercise and totally different to small boat handling. The crew had to take it in turns on the wheel and when the lifebuoy was thrown over and the shout of man overboard, Starboard or Port side, the action was to turn 30 degrees one way, then hard over the other way and finally 30 degrees the opposite way or something like that. The whole operation was supposed to take two minutes or more, which sometimes took us back to the buoy, sometimes not. There was one other factor that was not taken into consideration, the state of the weather. After trying all the crew except myself I then asked him if he had finished and was told that he had, so I now took over the wheel again and told him to time this as he had the other times. I then waited for the crew to shout man overboard again, when that happened I just came full astern back to the buoy and recovered it in twenty-five seconds. I then told him, 'That's the way to pick up that man.' 'But you may not be able to do that in bad weather,' says he. I then asked if he was likely to be with us if this situation occurred, 'Possibly not' was the answer, to which I replied that I most likely would be and I would be the one to decide when and how I could do it. So my attitude to these sorts of exercises was that if the crew were worth their salt they would know far better than anyone sitting behind a desk thinking up brilliant exercises.

We had a similar game one time, over the kind of knot that was used to fasten the hauling ropes to the buoy. At the time I was as usual in the wheelhouse watching what was going on. After a while I could see that there was quite a heated argument developing so I went to the foredeck and asked what the trouble was. One of the older members of the crew turned to me saying, 'He says this is the wrong knot for the breeches buoy, and it should be a double sheet bend. The last one said it should be this, a round turn and two half hitches, so I wish they would make up their bloody minds'. Again, in a very condescending manner, I asked this inspector if he was likely to be with us if we ever used the breeches buoy, 'Well possibly not' was the answer. I replied, 'Most likely not, but I most likely will be' (the changing tone) 'And I won't know and won't give a damn which knot they use, but I do know that the one they use will certainly not come adrift, and that's all I care.' – so that sorted that argument out.

After reading through my story, I feel that some people may get the impression that I was continually falling out with the Inspectors and those from Head Office, but this was not so. I made many good friends, but as I was not an employed man I could speak my mind without fear of the sack. Most of them listened and accepted what I was saying because of my whole life having been spent in and around boats and life saving. The others are not worth worrying about!!

One of my biggest worries while I was the Coxswain was that when we had a slipway boat, there was roughly speaking up to two hours over each low water, on the spring tide every fortnight when we were unable to launch, or may hit the bottom and be thrown back, side on to the slipway especially if there was a heavy sea running, but if I decided that I would not be able to launch, would some say it was because we didn't like the weather? I was very lucky, on several occasions we hit the bottom and on one trip I knew it was really risky. The weather was right onto the slipway; I had her lowered well down so that her forefoot would not dig in and when it was right shouted to let go. The boat got off the slip and did not dig in but was certainly dragging her keel on the bottom and gradually came to a stop, but luckily with the next wave she lifted and started slowly ahead again, and gathered way until we were off.

The only time we were wanted and were not able to attempt a launch for at least an hour, was a fine but foggy evening when a local boat had not returned from an evening's fishing. Just as I had decided that the tide was now high enough, the telephone rang telling us that the fishing party had returned to a different part of the Island and there was no need to launch, so everyone was happy.

I had a great surprise one day when I answered the telephone, and after asking my name a woman informed me that she was from a television programme called Gardener's World. She said that they had been told that we had a very nice colourful garden and they would like to come to make a programme about it. I just laughed and said that they must have got me mixed up with my brother. 'Oh no.' she said, 'It's you we want.' 'But I don't know one flower from another when it comes to names, and in any case I only really like growing veg or something to eat,' says I. 'Oh you have an allotment as well, have you?' was the next question. I had to admit to this, also that although we only have a back yard, in the summer it is quite colourful, but it is only that way because if there is a bit of a space I just shove something in it to fill it up, no matter what it is, as long as it has colour. 'Well can we come and see you early in the year?' – again I tried to put them off saying that there would be nothing to see, early in the year. There was no putting them off and sure enough they arrived with all their gear. Luckily the early potatoes were well under way and I had a few plants from my own seed that were big enough to dig, the beans, lettuce, shallots, onions etc. were just getting going, so the T.V. people were delighted with their filming and many people must, like myself have had a good laugh to see me on Gardener's World. I have the stainless steel trowel with the name on it to mark the occasion, it still makes me smile when I think of it, but several people phoned or wrote to me and said that they enjoyed it, so who dares wins, I suppose.

After having an attack of shingles I decided to try my hand at oil painting to pass away the time. In my time at school there was no such thing as art teachers, but I liked drawing from as far back as I can remember. In charge of one of the school classes that I passed through, was Bill Potter a very well liked and good teacher, he also was very good at drawing lessons and I always managed to get top marks for drawing. We were having a drawing lesson one time when Guthrie again was sitting next to me, we were allowed to draw whatever we wanted on this occasion but it had to be just from our own imagination. I decided to draw an aeroplane; it was just about finished when Bill came looking at our efforts. After looking at mine he looked at Guthrie's paper, on which there was only a dot in the middle, 'Where's your drawing?' he says. 'That's it Sir,' answers Guthrie, pointing to the spot on the paper. 'Well what do you mean? What is it?' asks Bill. 'It's Matt's aeroplane nearly out of sight Sir,' was the answer. I really can't remember what Mr. Potter actually said, but by his face he was having a job to keep control of his laughter and decided to show the class this latest great work of art.

To get back to my story I had never tried oil painting before but it seemed to be going reasonably well from the remarks I was getting from those that saw my efforts, especially the fishermen and locals as the paintings are all of boats or wrecks, except for one, which is of a Sunderland flying boat, and in my opinion one of the loveliest aircraft that ever flew. I afterwards turned to using Acrylic paints, really because I was too impatient, and could not wait for the paint to dry, this I readily admit is a great fault of mine. I have plenty of patience to keep at anything until I think I've got it right, but when I have started something I have to keep at it until it is finished. I also tried my hand at another of my hobbies of my younger days, which is model making, and have made several models of the R.A.F. Air Sea Rescue boats that I was coxswain of during my time in the service. These models are all hand made out of blocks of wood as near to scale as possible and the fittings are also made from all sorts of bits and pieces, which gives me great pleasure on being able to say that I had made them.

Jemma is now at Essex University in Colchester and we look forward to when she comes home for a holiday. Rebecca and Thomas are both at Richard Lander School in Truro. Rebecca is following in my footsteps and is a Corporal with the A.T.C., 77 Squadron, Redruth, based at R.A.F. Portreath and Thomas plays football for a team in Camborne called the Holman's Tigers and is also hoping to join the Air Force cadets later this year.

Now that it is time for me to finish this story of some of my working life, I apologise to those that I have not mentioned and should have, and thank those that have put up with me over the years and have given me their help and support in many ways, especially to those that were with me in the lifeboat, and also to Jean and John, Lucy and Ken, Jemma, Rebecca and Thomas. My main thanks go of course to the one that made most of it possible, and put up with many very worrying nights, just listening to the wind and rain, or the fog signals, and in later times to what news she could get from the wireless signals, until she would know that we were now, as we used to say 'Back and Ready for Service', – the one and only Pat.

LIFEBOAT SERVICES CREWED/COXSWAINED BY

M LETHBRIDGE BEM

THE 'CUNARD' LIFEBOAT

1947

April 8th   Fishing vessel 'YVETTE', Camaret. Landed 8 and later put crew aboard

Oct 4th   'S.S. RADSTOCK', Bridgewater. Saved vessel and Rescued 7

1948

March 29th   Fishing Boat 'PEACEFUL', Scilly. Gave help

April 19th   'S.S. DUKE OF SPARTA', London. Gave help

June 26th   Fishing Vessel 'ENERGETIC', Porthleven. Landed 1 and a body

1951

Jan 7th   Landed a sick man from BISHOP ROCK LIGHTHOUSE

Sept 10th   'S.S. SCILLONIAN', St. Mary's. Landed 30 and gave help

1952

May 17th   Motor launch 'GANNET', St. Mary's. Gave help

1953

Sept 8th   SAILING BOAT. Saved 2 and boat

1955

Jan 21st   'S.S. MANDO', Panama. Saved crew of 25

Feb 5th   Tug 'WARDEN' of the Royal Navy. Landed 4 injured men

Mar 23rd   Fishing vessel 'REINE DE LA MERE' of Douarneney, France. Gave help

July 22nd   'S.S. PUNTA', Panama. Landed 20

July 23rd   'S.S. PUNTA', Panama. Landed 5

THE *'GUY AND CLARE HUNTER'* MOTOR LIFEBOAT SENT TO THE STATION IN DECEMBER 1955 THE COST OF THIS BOAT WAS DEFRAYED BY THE AMALGAMATION OF 7 LEGACIES

1956

Aug 8th	Fishing boat 'CORAL', St. Mary's. Gave help
Aug 17th	Motor boat 'ERIN', St. Mary's. Gave help

1957

Aug 10th	Two SAILING DINGHIES. Landed 4
Aug 10th	Motor boat 'THE DAWN'. Saved boat and 8

1958

June 25th	Fishing boat 'MEDUSE', Brest. Saved boat and 4
Sept 28th	Fishing boat 'PAMELA', St. Martins. Gave help
Oct 4th	Yacht 'MARY ANN', Aberystwyth. Saved boat and 2

1959

April 26th	Motor Tug 'HELEN M. MCALLISTER'. Saved boat and 9
May 29th	Trawler 'JOSE RAMON', San Sebastian. Gave help

1960

June 2nd	H.M. SUBM 'TRUMP'. Landed sick man

1961

March 9th	Trawler 'PETIT JEAN YVES'. Ashore Gugh. Landed 5
March 10th	Trawler 'PETIT JEAN YVES'. Refloated vessel and escorted to harbour
June 28th	French Trawler 'ENFANT DES HOULET'. Stood by vessel
Aug 11th	F.V. 'MARY ANN'. Gave help
Oct 31st	Small boat 'M.A.B.', St. Mary's. Escorted boat

1962

Jan 6th	Took a sick man to Penzance

1963

June 7th	Motor boat 'FHANTEE'. Gave help
Oct 6th	French trawler 'KETTY ET MICHOU', Camaret. Put pilot and doctor onboard
Dec 14th	Yacht 'SEARIGS'. Gave help

1964

Jan 6th	'S.S. EVA JEANETTE', Stockholm. Landed a sick man
July 7th	Trawler 'ROSELAND', Newlyn. Escorted boat
Sept 14th	Converted Lifeboat 'WARATAH'. Gave help

1965

March 9th	ROUND ISLAND LIGHTHOUSE. Landed a sick man

THE 'CUNARD' LIFEBOAT

Aug 2nd   Yacht 'SEA RANGER'. Gave help

THE 'GUY & CLARE HUNTER'

Oct 22nd   M.V. 'CONSTANCE BOWATER'. Landed a sick man
Nov 28th   Yacht 'BARRANQUILLA'. Gave help

1966
June 5th   M.F.V. 'SANU'. Rescued 4
July 31st   Yacht 'MOSHULU'. Escorted boat
Oct 31st   Freighter 'AKBARJAYANTI', Bombay. Took out a doctor

1967
Jan 22nd   M.V. 'BREE-HELLE', Rotterdam. Gave help
March 18th   Liberian Tanker 'TORREY CANYON', Monrovia. Stood by vessel,
                 transferred 14 to Trinity House Vessel 'STELLA' and rescued 9
March 20th   Liberian Tanker 'TORREY CANYON', Monrovia. Stood by vessel
May 22nd   Motor yacht 'BRAEMAR'. Saved boat and 19

LIFEBOAT 'THOMAS MC.GUNN'

July 22nd   Ketch 'NOVA ESPERO', Falmouth. Saved boat and 2

THE 'GUY & CLARE HUNTER'

Oct 13th   Landing Craft 'SALVOR'. Landed one

1968
April 6th   Injured man aboard French Trawler 'MENEZ KEROVIL'. Escorted vessel
Sept 6th   BISHOP ROCK LIGHTHOUSE. Landed a sick man
Sept 19th   'S.S. JULIA JEMAITE', Klaipeda. Landed a sick man
Sept 20th   H.M. SUBMARINE 'ASTUTE'. Landed a sick man
Oct 21st   Sick man aboard Tanker 'OSCILLA'. Landed a sick man thereby
                saving a life

1969
Jan 18th   M.V. 'FIRTH FISHER', Barrow. Escorted vessel
Jan 23rd   French trawler 'KRUGUEN'. Saved vessel and 6
April 25th   Motor Vessel 'GENIE', Monrovia. Landed a sick man
July 29th   French yacht 'LA LIBERTINE'. Saved yacht and 5
Sept 22nd   Yacht 'MIDSHIP-CA', Brest. Gave help

1970
Feb 21st   M.V. 'NORDANHAV', Sidkoping. Rescued 10
April 15th   M.V. 'POLEIRE', Famagusta. Gave help
April 16th   Injured man aboard M.V. 'THORBJORG', Grimstad. Stood by for helicopter
June 1st   M.V. 'QUEENSGARTH', London. Landed a sick man
July 9th   M.F.V. 'ASTHOR'. Gave help
Nov 24th   M.V. 'WIEBOLD BOHMER', Rotterdam. Escorted vessel

1971
Feb 6th   M.V. 'CAPTAIN MICHAEL', Syros. Landed a sick man

THE 'JESSIE LUMB' LIFEBOAT

Aug 10th   Yacht 'KOOMOOLOO'. Stood by boat
Aug 13th   French trawler 'LESURDIT'. Took out doctor

1972
Jan 1st   Injured man onboard M.V. 'TINLAND', Helsingborg. Took out doctor
Jan 16th   Trawler 'BERNARD DE PERGIN', L'Orient in tow of trawler
                'SUMATRA', Etel. Escorted vessels
March 11th   Yacht 'MORONEL', Littlehampton. Saved boat and 2

THE 'GUY & CLARE HUNTER'

June 20th	Sick man onboard Liberian Tanker 'PAM'. Landed a sick man
June 24th	Sick man onboard sailing frigate 'DARPOSMORSZA'. Stood by boat
July 20th	Small fishing boat. Landed 2
Sept 30th	Sick man onboard M.V. 'STAGHOUND', U.S.A. Landed a sick man thereby saving a life
Oct 2nd	Sick man onboard M.V. 'SEALAND GALAWAY', U.S.A. Landed a sick man

1973

April 25th	Yacht 'RICHARD DAVY'. Took out a doctor
Oct 13th	32' Yacht 'EVBIOTEK' Ymuiden, Netherlands. Gave help
Oct 21st	Sick man on SEVEN STONES LIGHTVESSEL. Landed a sick man
Oct 31st	French trawler 'ROZENNO', La Rochelle. Landed an injured man

1974

Jan 25th	Injured man onboard French trawler 'MARCEL COROLLER'. Gave help
April 2nd	40' Yacht 'KATH-ALAIN', France. Gave help
April 7th	Sick man onboard M.V. 'RATNA KIRTI', Calcutta. Gave help
May 21st	Sick man onboard M.V. 'RADHOST', Czechoslovakia. Landed a sick man
June 20th	M.F.V. 'ANJONICA', Newlyn. Saved vessel and 2
July 31st	Aux Yacht 'DAPHNE', France. Saved vessel and 2
Aug 2nd	M.F.V. 'BOY JAN', Penzance. Gave help

1975

June 25th	Sick man onboard cargo ship 'ZAKEPANE'. Landed a sick man
July 27th	Sick man onboard trawler 'ARAVIS'. Took out a doctor
July 31st	Injured man onboard Liberian ship 'COMOS DENEB'. Landed an injured man
Aug 1st	Lobster boat 'VENUS DES ISLES'. Rescued 3
Sept 12th	Yacht 'BATUENAUDER', France. Gave help

1976

Jan 31st	Trawler 'PARGO', Spain. Escorted vessel
Jan 31st	Trawler 'MERGO', Spain. Landed a sick man
June 22nd	Sailing dinghy. Saved boat
July 21st	Tanker 'TREFALCON LOGIC', Monrovia. Landed a sick man
Aug 20th	Yacht 'TAYEL II', France. Gave help
Sept 11th	Trawler 'PATRICE MIRIAM', France. Escorted vessel
Sept 29th	Trawler 'RA RAU', Rumania. Stood by vessel
Nov 15th	Tender to Sail Training Ship 'SIR WINSTON CHURCHILL'. Saved boat and 9
Nov 20th	Sick man onboard cargo vessel 'LADY JANE'. Landed a sick man

Nov 30th	Yacht 'SNOWGOOSE OF WIGHT'. Saved boat and 3
Dec 7th	Trimaran 'COCONUT', Plymouth. Saved boat and 5
Dec 15th	Catamaran 'AUSSIE TOMCAT'. Saved boat and 1

1977

| Feb 13th | Trawler 'ENFANT DE BRETAGNE', France. Gave help |

THE 'GERTRUDE' LIFEBOAT

Aug 24th	Yachts 'TERN AND KIM'. Saved two boats and 1
Aug 24th	Yacht 'BAGARREUR', France. Saved boat and 2
Oct 7th	Catamaran 'NOKOMIS', France. Saved boat and 3

THE 'GUY AND CLARE HUNTER'

1978

Feb 6th	Sick man onboard tanker 'INTERMAR PROGRESS', Monrovia. Took out a doctor and landed a sick man
June 3rd	Converted motor fishing vessel 'DEEP DIVER'. Gave help
June 19th	Cargo vessel 'MALLING', London. Landed a sick man
Aug 30th	Catamaran 'WESTERN REVELLER', Plymouth. Rescued 1
Oct 13th	Fishing Vessel 'SWAN DANCER', Scilly. Gave help
Oct 22nd	Injured man onboard cargo vessel 'DUMBAIA', Glasgow. Took out a doctor

1979

Feb 8th	Sick man onboard trawler 'NORSE', Hull. Took out a doctor
Apr 7th	Canoe. Saved boat
Apr 8th	Ore carrier 'ASPIDOFOROS', Greece. Landed a sick man
Apr 19th	Motor Fishing Vessel 'EMMA GOODEY', Falmouth. Gave help
May 22nd	Cargo vessel 'IBN KHALLIKAN',Kuwait. Took out a doctor and Landed a sick man
June 21st	Yacht 'ALCYONE', Portsmouth. Gave help
Aug 8th	Cargo vessel 'SURREYBROOK'. Took out a doctor and landed a sick man
Aug 14th	Yacht 'VICTRIDE', France. Escorted yacht
Aug 14th	Yacht 'PEGASUS'. Escorted yacht
Aug 14th	Yacht 'FESTINA TERTIA'. Saved boat and 6
Sept 9th	Trawler 'KORRIG'. Landed an injured man

1980

| July 12th | Vessel 'SKELLIC ROCK', Cork. Landed a sick man |

THE 'ROBERT EDGAR' LIFEBOAT
SENT TO STATION ON 1st JULY 1981.
THIS LIFEBOAT WAS PROVIDED FROM THE GENEROUS GIFTS OF MRS ESME EDGAR AND MR A EDGAR

1981
Aug 31st	Capsized sailing dinghy. Saved boat
Aug 31st	French trawler 'AMADIS'. Stood by vessel
Dec 20th	PENLEE LIFEBOAT 'SOLOMON BROWNE'. Recovered wreckage
Dec 24th	Sick man onboard bulk carrier 'BISCHOFSTOR', West Germany. Took out doctor and landed a sick man

1982
Apr 4th	Yacht 'GINGEMBRE', France. Escorted boat
June 22nd	Yacht 'CONCHERTO'. Rescued 2
Aug 5th	Injured man onboard tanker 'AMMERSBEK',West Germany. Took out doctor and landed injured man

1983
Apr 2nd	Fishing boat. Saved boat and 1
Apr 2nd	Ferry 'ARMORIQUE', France. Escorted vessel
Apr 24th	Yacht 'NANOU', France. Saved boat and 3

THE 'SIR MAX AITKIN' LIFEBOAT
June 7th	Fishing boat 'JULIE ANNE', Penzance. Gave help
July 1st	Cabin cruiser 'SOUL SEARCHER', Belfast. Gave help
July 10th	Yacht 'KINGS RANSOME'. Saved boat and 2
July 16th	HELICOPTER. Rescued 6
Aug 1st	Yacht 'ELEANORA'. Saved boat and 4
Aug 5th	Injured man onboard trawler 'NUEVO EBENECER', Spain. Took out doctor and landed an injured man
Aug 6th	Injured man onboard trawler 'NUEVO EBENECER', Spain. Took out doctor and landed an injured man

THE 'ROBERT EDGAR' LIFEBOAT

Aug 24th	Trawler 'VAULTOUR', Lovient. Gave help
Sept 16th	Yacht 'PATNA', Poole. Gave help
Sept 19th	Injured man onboard M.F.V.'GRAN MARINELA', Spain. Landed an injured man
Oct 16th	Injured man onboard trawler 'NUEVO EBENECER', Spain. Took out doctor and landed an injured man
Oct 28th	Fishing vessel 'ROUANEZ LOCTUDY', France. Gave help

1984

May 6th	Catamaran 'FLYING HART', Yarmouth. Saved boat and 2
May 22nd	Yacht 'ZINGANA', Fleetwood. Rescued 4
July 29th	Yacht 'WILD GOOSE'. Saved boat and 2

RETIRED 20TH JANUARY 1985

'Robert Edgar' leaving harbour on service.

Left to right: Grandad Lethbridge and Dad taken on Grandad's retirement.

Dad and Myself taken on Dad's retirement.

*Lifeboat crew in the Sixties – left to right back row: Wilfred Woodcock, Jim Lethbridge Jnr.,
Richard Lethbridge, Bill Burrow, Harry Lethbridge, Engineer Inspector, Dr. Bell, Waldron Phillips.
Left to right front row: Rodney Terry, Freddy Woodcock, Myself, Roy Guy, Dad.*

*Lifeboat crew with the B.B.C. men taken off the Bishop Rock Lighthouse.
Left to right standing: Mr. Moyle, Uncle Jim, Harry, Charlie Coombs, Edward Ward, Myself,
Waldron Phillips, Roy Jenkins, Bert Jenkins.
Left to right kneeling: Henry Thomas, Richard, Dad.*

'Titch and Lofty' Weston-super-Mare 1942.

Learning the Trade.

Myself far left – Abidjan 1944.

R.N.L.I. AWARDS

1955

2nd Coxswains Certificate for service to the 'Mando' 21st January.

1967

A framed letter of appreciation, signed by the Chairman of the Institution, was sent to the Coxswain Matthew Lethbridge Jnr and crew for the services rendered to the tanker 'Torrey Canyon' of Monrovia, which went aground on the Seven Stones on 18th March.

Silver Medal awarded to Coxswain Matthew Lethbridge Jnr, Bronze Medals to Second Coxswain Ernest Guy and Motor Mechanic William Burrow and the Thanks of the Institution inscribed on Vellum were accorded to the remainder of the crew for rescuing the crew of 19 and saving the yacht 'Braemar' on 22nd/23rd May.

1970

Second Silver medal awarded to Coxswain Matthew Lethbridge Jnr. Second Bronze medal Second Coxswain Ernest Guy and Motor Mechanic William Burrow and the Thanks of the Institution inscribed on Vellum awarded to the remainder of the crew for the rescue of ten persons from the Swedish motor vessel 'Nordanhav' on 21st February.

1972

The Thanks of the Institution inscribed on Vellum accorded to Coxswain Matthew Lethbridge and crew member Rodney Terry when the lifeboat saved the yacht 'Moronel' and the crew of two 15 miles South East of St. Mary's on 11th March.

1977

Third Silver medal awarded to Coxswain Matthew Lethbridge BEM when the lifeboat made repeated attempts to reach the crew on board the French trawler 'Enfant de Bretagne', and then searched for survivors amongst many uncharted rocks in the darkness of the early hours of 13th February. The Thanks of the Institution inscribed on Vellum were accorded to the other members of the crew.

1979

A special framed certificate awarded to Coxswain and crew for display at the station in recognition of their services in connection with various yachts in difficulties during the Fastnet Race on 14th August.

1982

The Thanks of the Institution inscribed on Vellum accorded to Coxswain Matthew Lethbridge BEM when the lifeboat 'Robert Edgar' rescued the crew of two of the yacht 'Concherto' on 22nd June.

1983

The Thanks of the Institution inscribed on Vellum accorded to Coxswain Matthew Lethbridge BEM when the lifeboat 'Sir Max Aitken' on temporary duty at St. Marys, rescued six people from the water on 16th July after a helicopter had crashed in dense fog.